The Art of War and Enterprise Strategy Management

The Art of War and Enterprise Strategy Management

Fu Shouzhi

NA
NorthAmerican
Business Press

Atlanta – Seattle – South Florida - Toronto

North American Business Press, Inc

Atlanta, Georgia

Seattle, Washington

South Florida

Toronto, Canada

The Art of War and Enterprise Strategy Management

ISBN: 9780988919341

© 2013 All Rights Reserved.

Along with trade books for various business disciplines, the North American Business Press also publishes a variety of academic-peer reviewed journals.

Library of Congress Control Number: 2013932955

Library of Congress

Cataloging in Publication Division

101 Independence Ave., SE

Washington, DC 20540-4320

Printed in theUnited States of America

First Edition: 9780988919341

CONTENTS

PREFACE I

The Art of War is a world-known treasure in military science.

A real classic of wisdom can transcend fields, territories and even time and space. *The Art of War* by Sun Tzu is such an immortal work. By reading this book, we cannot only experience the profound Chinese culture but also get inspiration from the wisdom it includes.

The original text of *The Art of War* is composed of 13 chapters in over 6000 words. Each chapter attaches special importance to a specific military strategy. However, these chapters should not be understood separately, not to mention to be quoted out of context for it will destroy the organic system of strategies in this book. This book is a reflection of the military thought of Sun Tzu, summarizes a universal law from rich war experience and presents the strategic thinking and tactical principles of war.

Sun Wu is a native of the State of Qi during the late Spring and Autumn Period (now native of Huimin County, Shandong Province). After the civil unrest broke out in Qi, The Suns moved to the southern part of Wu and settled down in a country estate about 10 li (5km) west of the capital of Wu. Sun Wu grew up by playing military games with his little companions in farmlands intersected with waterways. Expecting Sun Wu to follow in the footsteps of the elders to be a militarist, his parents taught him the way to manage the state and military, military tactics, strategic thinking, trickery, and methods of using spies. Having mastered these, Sun Wu summarized all the war experience and theories passed down by the elders into *The Art of War,* a crystallization of wisdom that covers the military tactics of hundreds of years.

Recommended by Wu Tzu-hsu, Sun Wu came to visit He Lv, King of Wu, and presented him with *The Art of War* composed of 13 chapters. *The Art of War* was an eye-opener for He Lv and he ordered Sun Wu to train 180 maids in the imperial palace, from which He Lv discovered Sun Wu's talent in managing people and military. Thus He Lv named Sun Wu his general under whose training the army of Wu soon became a well-trained, highly-disciplined and powerful one. In 506 B.C., He Lv went out for battle himself, with Sun Wu his great general, leading 30,000 soldiers to fight 200,000 soldiers of the State of Chu. Under Sun's guidance, the Wu army won all the five battles, captured the capital city of Ying and defeated the powerful state of Chu. In 482 B.C., Sun led the Wu army to fight the State

1

of Jin and won, bringing Wu to its heyday. *Records of the Grand Historian·Collected Biographies of Sun Wu and Wu Qi* summed Sun's achievements as follows: "In the west, he defeated the Chu State and forced his way into Ying, the capital; to the north he put fear into the States of Qi and Jin, and spread his fame abroad amongst the feudal princes. And Sun Tzu shared in the might of the King."

The Art of War is rich in content, original in its opinions on basic issues related to war and army and flexible in strategies, tactics, operational principles and methods to manage the army. It raises five fundamental factors that decide the outcome of war: politics, right time, favorable location, commander and law, among which the primary factor is politics. Sun Tzu proposed many outstanding perceptions: "if you know your enemies and know yourself, you can win a hundred battles without a single loss," "attack where he is unprepared; take action when it is unexpected," "To subdue the enemy without fighting is the supreme excellence." In terms of the way to manage the army, he advocated that "soldier must be treated in the first instance with humanity, but kept under control by iron discipline." And the book also proposed specific ways to ensure knowing your enemies and yourself, such as "carry military supplies from the homeland and make up for their provisions relying on the enemy," "the soldier works out his victory in accordance with the situation of the enemy" "using five sorts of spies." As only with a comprehensive knowledge of your own situation and the situation of your enemies can you predict the outcome of war, it requires to know and compare before the war all the factors that will influence the outcome of war to find out your possibility of winning a war, which is a reflection of naive materialism. The book also puts forward that the laws of military operations are like water that is impossible to predict its way. Only by flexible operations of extraordinary and normal forces can one control the war. Advance and retreat, superior and inferior, strong and weak, weakness and strength, a large force and a few men are all relative words. "If you know your enemies and know yourself, you can win a hundred battles without a single loss," "apparent disorder is born of order; apparent cowardice, of courage; apparent weakness, of strength," "catch an enemy off guard with a surprise attack," "avoid the enemy's strength and strike his weakness" are vivid reflections of the essence of military dialectics.

As the cradle of *The Art of War* and homeland of sages, China should conduct a deep and systematic study of this immortal masterpiece of strategies to help more readers to understand the splendid Chinese ancient military culture and enhance the national confidence and sense of pride, thus activating the national spirit. We should be of one heart and mind to learn from the great wisdom and strategies in the book to make the past serve the present, directing enterprise management to develop productivity and thus help build an innovation-oriented socialist country with Chinese characteristics. Since the introduction of the reform and opening-up policy thirty years ago, the thought of dialectical materialism in *The Art of War,* crystallization of our ancient philosophical wisdom, permeates everywhere, from home to abroad, from the innovation and development in science and technology, the implementation of the strategies in enterprise management to international diplomatic strategies and the competition in business war.

As a naturalist scientist, Comrade Fu Shouzhi has made plentiful scientific achievements through a long time of scientific research and practice. He said that all his achievements benefited from *The Art of War*. In his spare time, Fu consciously applied the dialectical thoughts and military strategies to the enterprise management and business war in real-life cases. Now he has written *The Art of War and Enterprise Strategy Management* to help readers to appreciate the great wisdom of Sun Tzu and also to broaden businessmen's horizons of enterprise strategies so that they can make innovations in enterprise management and promote the development of productivity.

To practice the scientific outlook on development to develop advanced productive forces, we must discriminatingly inherit and carry forward our country's precious cultural heritage, develop out of carrying forward, make innovations out of development and make achievements out of innovation. The publication of this book can inspire people to discuss the latest achievements in enterprise management in a broader context and make greater contributions to accelerating the development of productivity.

I'd like to take this opportunity to express my sincere hope that experts, scholars and learned men with keen interest in productivity can, by studying how to strengthen enterprise management from different aspects and in different fields, beat a new track to accelerate the development of productivity. Only by allowing a hundred flowers bloom can a garden be full of the beauty of spring and usher in a more colorful spring of great development of productivity.

Wang Maolin
President and Academician of the Chinese Association of Productivity Science
April 10, 2010

PREFACE II

The essence of art of war--- conquer without a single fight

The Art of War is a gem in human military cultural heritage.

The Art of War incisively discusses the logical implication of "Tao, Heaven, Earth, Commander and Doctrine" and makes correct analytical judgment of the outcome of war. Its success of being spread through the ages lies in its rich content, exquisite discussion, profound thought and excellent strategies. It has been praised highly by strategists at home and abroad. As a national essence and a world's treasure, *The Art of War* is already a world-renowned military masterpiece. It was introduced to Japan in the 8th century and to Europe in the 18th century. Now it has been translated into 29 languages and spread all over the world. There are economics courses specializing in *The Art of War* in the United States, the book is a compulsory course of business majors in Japan, the West Point lists it as a compulsory military course, the new translation of *The Art of War* published in the Soviet Union has been passed down in Russia and British Field Marshal Montgomery called on all the military academies in the world to list *The Art of War* as a compulsory course.

Nowadays, the esteem, spread, study and application of The Art of War are still in the ascendant. The essence of art of war is to conquer without a single fight. What is more important is how to look for "Blue Ocean", guide and build a harmonious world. And the effect of art of war endows the age with new functions.

Comrade Fu Shouzhi makes use of the past to serve the present, gets rid of the stale and brings forth the fresh. He has extended the strategies in *The Art of War* into enterprise management and business war. By brainstorming and boldly trying to make innovations in the scientific research led by him, he has successfully improved the economic benefit of enterprises, making great contribution to the development of productivity, which is rare and commendable.

This book consists of the original text of The Art of War, notes, explanation, analysis, cases, illustrations, achievements and proverbs. Its rich content and plain language ensure it a good teaching material to study *The Art of War and Enterprise Strategy Management*. It will certainly be a good mentor to all businessmen.

If one studies the art of war, he knows how to act properly. If one loves the art of war, he is not militant. If one knows the art of war, he strives for peace.

I sincerely hope that the readers can read and understand this book with heart and then you will surely be clear and broad minded and the world will be at peace.

Chen Gui
Chinese Academy of Management Science
May 19, 2010, Beijing

FOREWORD

The Art of War Helps Me through Difficult times as an Entrepreneur

Start Business With Scraps Of Art Of War

As a fan of traditional Chinese culture, I have perused *The Book of Songs* and *The Analects of Confucius* in my youth. It was by accident that I came to read The Art of War. I saw the incomplete bamboo slips of The Art of War unearthed from Han Dynasty tombs published in newspaper. That is why I call it scraps of art of war. Despite its old age and incompletion, most parts of the book are well preserved and legible. I began to read the book carefully out of my love of ancient Chinese prose. Sun Tzu said: "If you know your enemies and know yourself, you can win a hundred battles without a single loss," "Therefore, the outcome of a war is governed by five constant factors. To make assessment of the outcome of a war, one must compare the various conditions of the antagonistic sides in terms of these five constant factors: (1) Tao; (2) Heaven; (3) Earth; (4) Commander; (5) Doctrine." Suddenly, I was enlightened: no matter what you do, if you want to succeed, you have to assess it with the five constant factors. As long as the five constant factors are ready, one can surely succeed. The five constant factors are political stability, right time, favorable location, support of people and law. With the five factors at hand and knowing your enemies and yourself, you will surely make great achievements. Thus, *The Art of War* became tightly bound with my opening up my cause.

In early 1990s (right time), the reform and opening up policy was deepened in China (political stability). Inspired by *The Art of War*, I conceived the idea of establishing a business. At that time, the intellectual resources were rich in Dalian Jiaotong University (favorable location). It can be said that everything is in order except what is crucial for there are many "soldiers and commanders." Under the support of Dalian Municipal Science and Technology Commission (law), Dalian Katelin Specific Alloy Institutes affiliated to Dalian Jiaotong University was set up. My first step to establish a business---the examination and approval by Dalian Municipal government--- was very smooth.

However, at the initial stage of establishing a business, it was beset with difficulties for there was no capital, no equipment and no workshops. As we had no capital, we were forced to rely on loans the annual interest of which was more than 200,000 yuan, which was an enormous pressure for me. But no matter how great the difficulties might be, I had to stick it out for there was no way back. In retrospect, difficulty is the teacher of success. It is by being enlightened by *The Art of War* that I started on my difficult journey as an entrepreneur. And finally, I had overcome all the unimaginable difficulties.

The Art Of War Helps Me Out

Sun Tzu said that "the law of successful operations is to avoid the enemy's strength and strike his weakness." When Dalian Katelin Specific Alloy Institute was just founded, it was weak in foundation and short in capital. So in order to get out of the trouble early, we had to rely on ourselves and make use of our innovative technologies, which adopted the strategic principle of "avoid the strength and strike the weakness."

We temporarily avoided large enterprises with great technical strength and targeted our technical service at relatively weak SMEs and township enterprises, which has received unexpected effects. At that time, the brickyards and cement plants that had spread all over were in dire need of our wear resistance technology and thus were very glad to be served by us. There was great scope for the wear-resistant gold dust and welding rod and the wear-resistant alloy spraying process we had developed in township enterprises such as brickyards and cement plants. By using our wear resistance technology, the life of building materials and equipment had been prolonged, the product quality had improved, the output had increased and the cost had decreased. Soon our technologies were spread all over the township enterprises and for a time, the supply of wear resistance products fell short of the demand.

Everyday people from township enterprises came to buy our wear resistance materials, which became our sources of revenues, brought abundant start-up capital to pay off the bank loan and thus got us out of trouble and brought new opportunities to the great development of our institute. The strategic thinking of "knowing your enemies and yourself" and "avoid the strength and strike the weakness" turned "the double weakness" into "double strengths," making our institute win victory in our the first battle.

Forge Ahead And Set Sail

Sun Tzu said: "the general who thoroughly understands the advantages that accompany variation of tactics knows how to employ troops." The variations of tactics put forward by Sun Tzu have summarized the law of the growth of things. Everything develops out of changes and blaze new trails out of development, which is the universal law of the development of cause. And our institute develops following this law. Making innovations during its growth ensures the invincibility of an enterprise.

Enlightened by The Art of War and under the guidance of the scientific outlook on development, the institute carried out the "four strategies" (talent strategy, scientific and technical innovation strategy, market development strategy and enterprise management strategy), an enterprise management innovation. By doing so, the institute had ascended on the "four steps" of scientific and technical innovation, solved the wear resistance problems of brick machines, the top of shaft kiln unloading tower in cement plants, the fan propeller in large enterprises, large-scale equipment of thermoelectricity, electricity generation, nuclear power, metallurgy, machinery, petrifaction and military weaponry.

The firm four steps enabled the institute to expand its size gradually and contribute more to the nation. We translated our science and technologies into powerful productive forces across the country, had created billions of yuan for the country, with strong support for the development of our country. Now our institute is not the one it used to be. It is rich in talent resources: eight academicians, professors, senior engineers and doctors and 30 technicians. It also has its own intellectual property, many invention patents and four high-tech achievements, all of which have been translated into productive forces. Our service objects have changed from township enterprises to large state-owned enterprises and the service market has expanded to all provinces, cities and autonomous regions all over the country. Our first-class laboratories, factories and scientific research team enable the institute to design, produce and develop, which ensures its high product quality, new technologies, large market and saleability. Its annual output and profit and taxes doubles. Therefore, the institute has won over 10 national awards: Excellent Enterprise of China, Second Prize of National Scientific and Technological Progress, European "Eureka" Invention Award, Excellent People in China's Reform, Achievement of China's Enterprise Management Innovation, Scientific and Technological Invention of Dalian Municipal People's Government, and the sixth Outstanding Contribution to National Development of Productivity.

The achievements our institute has made today owe a lot to *The Art of War.*

Here is a poem to prove this:

By accident I read the art of war,

A mentor in my pursuit of great cause

Its strategies of great vision

Helps me prosper for a hundred years

If you want to know how to apply the great wisdom and strategies in *The Art of War* to directing the constant growth of enterprises, please read how I studied, understood and applied the thirteen chapters of *The Art of War*. This book presents my own journey as an entrepreneur, the achievements I have made and my own experiences for the references of entrepreneurs, in the hope that we can grow together and make greater contribution to the development of productivity.

The Art Of War And Enterprise Strategy Management

Nowadays, in order not to fail and lose the bearings in vast ocean of market economy and to advance at full speed according to its present goals, an excellent entrepreneur must have many capabilities, especially the capability to make the right decision about business strategies and correct judgment of the economic situation of market economy. And he must have a strategic vision that has the whole world in view. The series of strategic thoughts in *The Art of War* is quite helpful in improving an entrepreneur's quality and his ability to make strategic decisions and the capability of management, among which the strategic thinking is a valuable classic for the entrepreneurs to carefully study and follow and also the magic key to the success of enterprise. Only by carefully studying and practicing the strategic thoughts in the book can we really improve ourselves and realize its value.

In order to help the readers and the entrepreneurs who aim to show their talents in enterprise management to better understand the position and function of *The Art of War* in enterprise management and to flexibly apply it, this book presents the original text of *The Art of War.* Nevertheless, *The Art of War* is an integral organic strategy, only on the basis of which can one, combining the practice of enterprise management to learn from application and apply from learning, digest it and improve his strategic thinking in actual enterprise management. The purpose of learning is to use and the purpose of use is to better serve the development of productivity, the building of socialism with Chinese characteristics and the building of an innovation-oriented country.

The Art of War is an immortal masterpiece among Chinese or even the world's military works, the strategic thoughts of which are common magic keys for military strategists, businessmen and entrepreneurs. The best way to inherit and carry forward our country's valuable cultural heritage is to apply it in practice. Internationally, over 30 countries, such Japan, the US and even the West Europe, have not only used *The Art of War* as their military textbook but also listed it as the compulsory reading in diplomacy, enterprise management and business strategies. It may well be that *The Art of War* is a magic key to the success of enterprise management. My purpose to write this book is to inherit and carry forward our cultural heritage and to apply Sun Tzu's military strategic thoughts to enterprise management and strategies of business war. The book is based on the thirteen chapters of *The Art of War*. Each chapter of this book consists of the original text, notes, explanation, analysis and cases to present the value of *The Art of War* in enterprise management and to show the important role of the strategies of *The Art of War* in enterprise management through the successful development of Dalian Katelin Specific Alloy Institute.

Fu Shouzhi
Dalian Jiaotong University

INTRODUCTION

The Art of War is a bright gem of classic Chinese military cultural heritage and an important part of excellent traditional Chinese culture. The book covers a wide range of topics and its thought is profound and rich, written in a concise style and with rigorous logic. This book of thirteen chapters is a gift to Ho Lu, king of Wu, by Sun Wu at their first meeting. Now *The Art of War* has been translated into over 10 languages such as Japanese, English, French, German and Russian and spread all over the world. It is reputed "the founder of oriental strategies," "the world's first ancient book of the art of war" and "the canon of strategies."

This book is not only a valuable book leading to military victory but also a magic key to success in today's business war. The application of the great military strategies in the book in enterprise management can enlighten and inspire people, such as "the best way of using forces is laying plans," "if you know your enemies and know yourself, you can win a hundred battles without a single loss," "avoid the strength and strike the weakness," "make the devious route the most direct and to turn disadvantage to advantage," "use the normal force to engage and use the extraordinary to win," and "subdue the enemy without fighting." All these thoughts of great wisdom are of immeasurable value to successful enterprise management.

The Art of War and Enterprise Strategy Management is a comprehensive, systematic, specific and vivid summary of how Academician Fu Shouzhi studied and successfully applied *The Art of War* to manage his life and enterprise. By using the strategies in *The Art of War*, Fu not only made it to be an academician, but also led Dalian Katelin Specific Alloy Institute to leapfrog development which brought the country with billions of yuan and has won many honors. Using his own experience as cases, Fu vividly shares with us his valuable experience in how to apply the great strategies in *The Art of War* to enterprise management and make success.

The book contains the original text of *The Art of War*, notes, explanation, analysis, cases, illustrations, achievements and proverbs. Its rich content, combination of theories and practice, completion of text and pictures and plain language ensure it a good textbook to study *The Art of War and Enterprise Strategy Management*. It will surely become a mentor to all entrepreneurs, businessmen and managers.

Chapter 1
LAYING PLANS

"Laying plans" is the center of this chapter and also the soul of the art of war. The highest state of war is not to compete in forces but in wits. As the old saying goes, "A good strategy at home wins the battle a thousand miles away." The competition in forces on the battlefield is nothing but a continuation of the competition in wits.

The calculations in the temple in a war are very important, for the correctness of the calculations is the key to the victory of a war.

War[1] is a matter of vital importance to the State; a matter of life and death, the road either to survival or to ruin. Hence it is a subject of inquiry[2] which can on no account be neglected.

Therefore, the outcome of a war is governed by five constant factors[3]. To make assessment of the outcome of a war, one must compare the various conditions of the antagonistic sides[4] in terms of these five constant factors: (1) Tao[5]; (2) Heaven; (3) Earth; (4) Commander; (5) Doctrine.

1. Tao causes the people to be in complete accord with their ruler, so that they will follow him regardless of their lives, undismayed by any danger.

2. Heaven signifies yin and yang, cold and heat, times and seasons[6].

3. Earth comprises distances, great and small; danger and security; open ground and narrow passes; the chances of life and death.

4. Commander stands for the virtues of wisdom, sincerity, benevolence, courage and strictness.

5. By doctrine, it means *quzhi* (the marshalling of the army in its proper subdivisions), *guandao* (the graduations of rank among the officers), and *zhuyong*(the maintenance of roads by which supplies may reach the army and the control of military expenditure)[7].

These five constant factors should be familiar to every general. He who knows them will win; he who knows them not will be defeated.

Therefore, to forecast the outcome of a war, the attributes of the antagonistic sides should be analyzed by making the following comparisons: which of the two sovereigns possesses greater Tao? Which of the two commanders is more capable? Which side holds more favorable conditions derived from Heaven and Earth? On which side is discipline better implemented? Which army is stronger? On which side are officers and men better trained? Which side is stricter and more impartial in meting out rewards and punishments? By means of these seven comparisons, I can forecast victory or defeat.

If the sovereign heeds these strategies of mine[8] and acts upon them, he will surely win the war, and I shall, therefore, stay with him. If the sovereign neither heeds nor acts upon them, he will certainly suffer defeat, and I shall leave.

Having paid attention to the advantages of my strategies[9], the commander must create a helpful situation[10] over and beyond the ordinary rules. By "situation," I mean he should act expediently in accordance with what is advantageous in the field and so meet any exigency.

All warfare is based on deception[11]. Hence, when able to attack, we must seem unable; when using our forces, we must seem inactive; when we are near, we must make the enemy believe we are far away; when far away, we must make him believe we are near. Bait the enemy when he covets small advantages; strike the enemy when he is in disorder; take double precautions against the enemy if he is well prepared with substantial strength[12]. If the enemy is of choleric temper, seek to irritate him[13]. If the enemy appears humble[14], make him arrogant. If his forces are at ease[15], wear them down. If his forces are united, divide them. Attack where he is unprepared; take action when it is unexpected. These are the keys to victory for a strategist. However, they cannot be formulated in detail beforehand.

The reason why a victory can be forecasted during the calculations in the temple[16] before the war is that the strategies are carefully planned and the conditions of victory are enough[17] and vice versa. The army with more carefully planned strategies and more conditions of victory will win and the army with less carefully planned strategies and fewer conditions of victory will not. How much less chance of[18] victory has the army with no plan and conditions of victory at all! By examining the situation through these aspects, I can foresee who is likely to win or lose.

1.1 Notes

1. War: here means the army.

2. Inquiry: investigation and study. In old Chinese, the equivalent of inquiry not only means "being observant and alert" but also "trying to figure out the morale of the army".

3. ...the outcome of a war is governed by five constant factors: the Chinese equivalent of "governed" used in the original text is "经" (*Jing*, it means the warp yarns in weaving). The ancient Chinese believed that weaving warp yarns is the main task in weaving. Here warp yarns extends to the meaning of guiding principles. Five constant factors refer to "Tao, Heaven, Earth and Doctrine". They are the rules that must be observed by the military.

4. ...To make assessment of the outcome of a war, one must compare the various conditions of the antagonistic sides: to compare the plans of the two antagonistic sides so as to forecast the outcome of the war.

5. Tao: literally it means way and path. Here it is extended to mean political opinions.

6. ...yin and yang, cold and heat, times and seasons: yin and yang refers to day and night, and the change of weather. Cold and heat means the difference in temperature: cold or hot. Times and seasons means the alternation of the four seasons.

7. *Quzhi, guandao, zhuyong*: *qu* is a relatively small unit of ancient army formation. *Quzhi* is a system in terms of army formation. *Guandao* refers to the assignment of duties to the officers, the management form and system. *Zhu* means direct and take charge of. *Yong* is military expenditure, here means the supply management system of military materials, instrument and military expenditure.

8. If the sovereign heeds these strategies of mine: if King Wu takes my strategies.

9. Having paid attention to the advantages of my strategies...: the favorable military plan is already adopted, i.e., the military decision is already made.

10. Situation: here means circumstances and environments in the battlefield.

11. Deception: ways of cheating and hoodwinking.

12. ...well prepared with substantial strength: in well-designed battle formation and substantial weapons.

13. Irritate: provoke your opponent incessantly.

14. Humble: many people explain "humble" as "(we) use humble words". Yet in light of the feature of the pattern of the next sentence, the subject of "humble" should be the enemy, i.e. the enemy flinches or is very cautious.

15. ...at ease: here means that the enemy is taking a good rest.

16. The calculations in the temple: in ancient China, before sending troops to participate in a war, a ceremony would be held in the temple to make plans for the battle, forecast the outcome of the war and formulate strategies. This procedure of preparing for the war is called calculations in the temple.

17. The strategies are carefully planned and the conditions of victory are enough: thoroughly planed and thus has more likelihood of victory.

18. How much less chance of: not to mention.

1.2 Explanation

Sun Tzu said: War is of vital importance to a state, a matter of people's life and death, and a big issue concerning the state's survival or ruin. Therefore, it is imperative to investigate and study it thoroughly.

In order to find out the true conditions of the antagonistic sides, a comparative analysis needs to be made from five aspects. In a word, "if you know your enemies and know yourself, you can win a hundred battles without a single loss."

The first aspect is moral influence, the second weather, the third favorable location, the fourth commander and the fifth method and discipline. Moral influence, in terms of politics, is the common feelings of the people. If the people are in accord with the sovereign, it means the political line and the policies and guidelines are correct, so that the people will work hard side by side, regardless of the danger of death, and will be willing to serve the state. Such people of a state are invincible. Weather refers to day and night, fine days and rain, bitter cold and torrid heat, and the change of the four seasons in wartime. Favorable location means geographical conditions such as the wartime terrain, surface features, the distance between two armies, the steepness and smoothness of the terrain, its broadness and narrowness, a terrain of life or one of death. And commander means whether the commander of the army is resourceful, credible, and benevolent to his troops, brave and decisive, and strict with the military discipline. And method and discipline refer to the military formation, military training, daily education, military rules, weaponry and military supplies. The above five aspects should be at the fingertips of every commander. Only in this way can the victory be achieved.

That's why a comparison between the specific conditions of the antagonistic sides is needed to assess the outcome of the war: which of the two sovereigns is more liberated and implements correct policies? Which of the two commanders is wiser? Which side has more favorable time, weather and physical location? On which side is discipline better implemented? Which side has stronger military strength and better weaponry? On which side are officers and men better trained? Which side manages better and is stricter and more impartial in meting out rewards and punishments? By comparing the above factors, one can forecast which side will win the war.
If my strategies are adopted and used to direct the war, the victory is assured and I will stay. If not, the irrational use of military forces will inevitably lead to defeat, and I will leave.

If after weighing the advantages and disadvantages of my strategies, the commander considers my strategies feasible, he should seek to create a favorable situation to help the military action. By situation, it means to flexibly control the initiative of the war according to the principle of self-interest. That is to say, the right action derives from the right thought.

War is a deception. One needs to look one way and row another, create something out of nothing and hoodwink the enemy so that he becomes puzzled. When good at fighting, pretend to be weak and feeble; when planning to fight, pretend to not take any action; when planning to attack the target nearby, pretend to attack the target far away and vice versa. If the enemy is greedy, bait him with small benefits. If the enemy is in disorder, take the opportunity to attack him. If the enemy is strong, be carefully prepared. If he is superior in strength, evade him. If he is of choleric temper, seek to irritate him so that he may lose his head. If he appears humble, try to make him become arrogant. If his forces have taken a good rest, wear them down. If his forces are united, divide them.

Attack where he is unprepared; take action when it is unexpected. In these military devices lies the secret of a strategist's art of command. However, they cannot be rigidly formulated beforehand.

Before the war, when the headquarters are making plans, if the plans are well designed and the requirements of conditions are met, a victory can be forecast. Otherwise, it will be hard to achieve a victory. Not even to mention the outcome of no plan and no condition at all! We can, according to these conditions, forecast which side will win the war.

1.3 Analysis

"Laying plans" is the center of this chapter and also the soul of the art of war. The highest state of war is not to compete in forces but in wits. As the old saying goes, "A good strategy at home wins the battle a thousand miles away." The competition in forces on the battlefield is nothing but a continuation of the competition in wits. Tao, Heaven, Earth, Commander and Doctrine are the premises of strategies and the elements of war. On the premise of understanding these five elements, we make the following seven comparisons: which of the two sovereigns possesses greater Tao? Which of the two commanders is more capable? Which side holds more favorable conditions derived from Heaven and Earth? On which side is discipline better implemented? Which army is stronger? On which side are officers and men better trained? Which side is stricter and more impartial in meting out rewards and punishments? By means of these seven comparisons, we can come to the conclusion of on which side the army is stronger, which is the completion of the preparation of making strategies. However, the strategies of war are extremely mysterious. In order to confuse the enemy, we use the following strategies: when able to attack, we seem unable; when using our forces, we seem inactive; when we are near, we make the enemy believe we are far away; when far away, we make him believe we are near. Bait the enemy when he covets small advantages; strike the enemy when he is in disorder; take double precautions against the enemy if he is well prepared with substantial strength. If the enemy is of choleric temper, seek to irritate him. If the enemy appears humble, make him arrogant. If his forces are at ease, wear them down. If his forces are united, divide them. Attack where he is unprepared; take action when it is unexpected. These are the keys to victory for a strategist. However, they cannot be formulated in detail beforehand.

The calculations in the temple in a war are very important, for the correctness of the calculations is the key to the victory of a war.

Sun Tzu deems "Tao", i.e. politics, as the primary factor. He believes that only when the politics of the state wins the heart of the people and "makes the people in completely accord with their ruler" will people follow him regardless of their lives and undismayed by any danger. These viewpoints are the same with the reason why ideological and political work should be strengthened in the army today. The idea of "wisdom, sincerity, benevolence, courage and strictness" put forward by Sun Tzu is also a standard of choosing a commander today. It is the unified standard of being an excellent commander, entrepreneur and politician.

In comparison with Sun Tzu's Art of War, the basic law of business war and business management communicates with that of a real war. First of all, as an excellent entrepreneur, one has to be equipped with the five talents possessed by a military conductor: wisdom, sincerity, benevolence, courage and strictness. For different military strategists and entrepreneurs, these five talents are different, or each of them accounts for different proportions, rather.

Zhuge Liang, Zhou Yu and Cao Cao are all outstanding military strategists during the Three Kingdoms period. They differ in their ability to judge and the way of seeing things. Zhuge Liang can forecast, Zhou Yu can see the truth at the first sight of a thing, while Cao Cao is a man of hindsight.

When Sima Yi's army reached the city gate, Zhuge Liang knew that Sima Yi was a man of suspicion, and that he would not enter the city without deep thought. So Zhuge Liang ordered to open the city gate, deluding the enemy by presenting a bold front to conceal unpreparedness, while Zhuge Liang sang to the music played by himself on the fortress. Despite an empty city in front of him, Sima Yi dared not to enter it and ordered his army to retreat for thirty li (15km). This story shows Zhuge Liang's excellent judgment and great ability of mastering the inside situation of the enemy. This is called psychological warfare.

At the eve of a war, Cao Cao took advantage of the fact that Jiang Gan and Zhou Yu were classmates and sent Jiang Gan to Zhou Yu's army to obtain information on their military situation. At the sight of Jiang Gan, Zhou Yu realized that Jiang Gan was a spy sent by Cao Cao. Therefore, using the strategy of sowing discord among the enemy, Zhou Yu forged a letter of capitulation under the name of Cao Cao's two navy generals Cai Mao and Zhang Yun, put it on the table and intentionally got drunk and gave Jiang Gan the opportunity to steal the letter to get the "inside information" of Zhou's military situation.

When Jiang Gan discovered the Capitulation, he felt as if he had found a treasure. So he brought the letter back to Cao's camp the very night. Seeing the Capitulation by his two generals, Cao got into rage and ordered to decapitate the two navy generals outside the camp's gate. Soon after the decapitation Cao Cao came to realize that he had fallen in to the trap set by Zhou Yu. Despite this, it was already too late.

In the complex business war, no smart entrepreneur can predict everything with miraculous accuracy. It is not easy even to predict the general tendency. People like Zhuge Liang who is such a proficient prophet are very few in our real life, or it is just a state that people long for. However, as an outstanding entrepreneur, one has to be strict with himself and try to make as few mistakes as possible or no mistakes at all.

Thus, "governing with five constant factors" and "making seven comparisons" in business management communicate with those in military. The five constant factors in management are: people's heart, law, environment, talent and rule.

People's heart: the blue blood spirit of the army. The Chinese saying goes that when people work with one mind, they can even remove Mount Tai. Only when all the employees work with one mind and devote themselves to the enterprise can it turn from weak to strong.

Law: everything has its law of development, so does an enterprise in its course of growing from small to large and turning from weak to strong. To follow the law of development is to do things according to the scientific outlook on development. Only by means of constant reform and innovation can an enterprise continuously win in the competition.

Environment: the geographical location of an enterprise. Whether it has convenient transportation, abundant natural resources and capital, developed human environment and culture, rich human resources and intelligence resources, harmonious social environment and society, affluent and stable people's lives, and whether it is supported by the government. All these are important factors affecting the healthy development of an enterprise and indispensable factors in victory.

Talent: people are the most active factor and the fundamental element in productivity. As employees in an enterprise, they have to be equipped with certain qualities, including intelligence, sincerity, benevolence, courage and self-discipline. Only by being equipped with these five qualities can they fulfil the task of the team.

Rule: an enterprise must have sound rules and regulations, safety system, job operating duty and responsibility system.

The above five constant factors and those in Sun Tzu's Art of War supplement each other.

The seven comparisons are: Does the team have clear goals?

Does the entrepreneur have strong leadership skills?

Is he familiar with the environment and does he master the law to do business?

Is there any law he follows to do business?

Does the team have strong execution?

Are the team members proficient in their respective work?

Is the enterprise strict and impartial in meting out rewards and punishments?

From the above seven aspects, it is easy to predict whether the enterprise can win the competition.

1.4 Cases

Case 1

According to the features of Dalian Katelin Specific Alloy Institute (hereinafter referred to as our institute) that there are a lot of young people, and to satisfy the job need, a military formation is adopted, three people in a group, five in a team with a headman and a team leader respectively. Each team serves as a work unit. The team leader is not only responsible for the job of the whole team but also works as the team's safety supervisor. In order to establish his authority in the team, the team leader is required to be proficient in his job, set an example for all the team members in performing the tasks given by the institute and take into account the production costs and profits.

Our institute provides the personnel with uniforms, even backpacks. On arriving at our institute, the new employees have the feeling of "joining the army" for we make use of the intervals between working time to make them experience "military training," mainly in the purpose of enhancing their sense of organizational discipline. Through queue training, we try to foster their collective spirit and basic quality of a soldier. Just as what is written in Sun Tzu's Art of War, only a man with a soldier's quality can have strong fighting capacity and execution.

Our institute also organizes our personnel to follow West Point, laying great emphasis on the development of "personality charm", for the people our personnel contact outside our institute are leaders of high level, such as factory manager, general manager, chief engineer and workshop director. While dealing with these people, our personnel have to fully demonstrate their cultural awareness and personality charm, which requires them to be a high quality person with good technical skills.

It is due to that our institute has closely combined business management with military management that we have trained high-quality personnel. They are hard-working and faithfully carry out the mission statement made by the institute: "Don't mention the difficulties met in your job, for you are meant to solve these difficulties." When the conditions exist, complete the job well and when the conditions do not exist, create conditions to complete the job. This has already become a conscious action of all the personnel and their tenacity has touched our clients many times. For instance, once we sent two employees to perform a task in Tiansheng Thermal Power Plant. Due to the tight project time and heavy task, they work overtime for

24

consecutive nights, not taking a rest even when they got bloodshot eyes until they finished the task with quality and quantity assured. Their spirit and action had moved the leaders of the plant who suggested us for many times to award them for their high-quality work, fast speed and short construction period.

Another example is performing a task in Jilin Thermal Power Plant. There were three units before us that had made a field investigation at the construction site and all refused to undertake the task for the site is too narrow. At last, the plant came to our institute. After doing a careful investigation at the site, we proposed the principle of choosing the right person for the right task. As the site is narrow, we sent thin and small yet flexible employees to perform the task. They had overcome all the difficulties and finally successfully accomplished the task. The plant was deeply moved and complemented our institute: "Your institute is great. Your employees can overcome various difficulties and accomplish all different kinds of task."

Case 2

An excellent scientific and technical worker should be equipped with the five characters of a commander---wisdom, sincerity, benevolence, courage and strictness and practice the scientific outlook on development to develop the national science and technology, which is also "a matter of vital importance to the State; a matter of life and death, the road either to survival or to ruin and hence a subject of inquiry which can on no account be neglected," for the history has taught us that backwardness leaves you vulnerable to attack.
Only by being guided by this thought can we scientific researchers connect our scientific researches with the prosperity of our country. The reason why we can make so many fast achievements lies in that we use this thought to educate our employees to mobilize their initiative and creativity to the greatest extent.

"The commander who gets few scores during the calculations in the temple before the war will have less chance of success. With many scores, one can win; with few scores, one cannot. How much less chance of victory has one who gets no scores at all! By examining the situation through these aspects, I can foresee who is likely to win or lose." A famous Chinese saying goes that neither eating nor clothing brings you poverty, but your living without planning. With this idea in mind, every successful achievement in scientific research is made through elaborate planning and research.

First of all, we find subject from production practice. The difficulty in production is the best subject of our scientific research. The CFB boiler adopts advanced technologies introduced from foreign countries and high in thermal efficiency. But its deadly weakness is its serious abrasion which always cause pipe burst and pipe leakage that brought great loss to the production of thermal electricity and heating in winter.

According to the strategy of "know your enemy and know yourself, you will win a hundred battle without a single loss" in *The Art of War*, we need to conduct a careful study and research to find the cause of serious abrasion and the way to reduce it. Seeing from the operation principle of the CFB boiler, the floating up and down of the coal bed and the flow of the coal bed caused by the primary and the secondary air enforce the firing effect. However, it also increases the abrasion against the water wall tube, the primary cause of the abrasion and leakage of boiler pipe. If it is fast, it only takes one month for the pipe burst and leakage to happen. If it is slow, it takes three to four months. The pipe burst and leakage will cut off steam and suspend production, severely threatening the electricity generation and heating in winter. By investigating the "situation of the enemy," we have found the cause and location of serious abrasion, which can be said "knowing your enemy." But this is far from enough. We need to know ourselves: what measures should be taken to get rid of the hidden trouble?

The first approach is to add anti-wear protection tiles. But its defect is that it will influence the heat transfer, reduce the thermal efficiency and consume more energy.

The second approach is hot spray wielding. It will transform the base metal and the deformation of the tube will increase the abrasion of vortex.

We adopted the third approach: to cold flame plate wear resistant alloy on water wall tube. By doing so, the surface hardness was reinforced and the hidden trouble caused by vortex abrasion was eliminated, prolonging the lifespan of the boiler tube more than three times. The bottleneck problem of thermal electricity generation was soon solved, which has brought benefits to national energy conservation, emission reduction, increased production and saved cost, and thus has won the national invention patent.

In fact conducting scientific research and fighting are the same. It is hard to invent and create without analyzing technical difficulties and understanding what your advantages are. "Know your enemy and know yourself" has helped us to successfully combine our invention patent with production practice and soon translated the patent into productive forces. Our patented technology has been widely applied in power plants and thermal power plants all over the country, bringing great economic and social benefits worth billions of yuan to hundreds of enterprises. Our patent number is ZL01102869.6.

It is hard to predict what disaster or disease will strike us down. So try to seize the time to do good for people when we are still alive and healthy.

-Author's note

Chapter 2
WAGING WAR

"What is valued in war is a quick victory, not prolonged operations" is an important operational principle raised in this chapter. Any war is a great consumption of human resources, material resources and financial resources. Thus, the longer a war is, the more harmful is to the national economy and the people's livelihood. In light of this, Sun Tzu advocated that "What is valued in war is a quick victory, not prolonged operations," which benefits the country's lasting political stability and peace.

Sun Tzu said: Generally, operations of war involve one thousand swift chariots[1], one thousand heavy chariots[2] and one hundred thousand mailed troops with the transportation[3] of provisions for them over a thousand miles. Thus the expenditure at home and in the field, the stipends for the entertainment of guests[4], the cost of materials such as glue and lacquer[5] and the expense for care and maintenance of chariots and armor, will amount to one thousand dollars a day. An army of one hundred thousand men can be raised only when this money is in hand. In directing such an enormous army, a speedy victory is the main object. If the war is long delayed, the men's weapons will be blunted and their ardor will be dampened. If the army attacks cities, their strength will be exhausted. Again, if the army engages in protracted campaigns[6], the resources of the state will not suffice. Now, when your weapons are blunted, your ardor dampened, your strength exhausted[7] and your treasure spent, neighboring rulers will take advantage of your distress to act. In this case, no man, however wise, is able to avert the disastrous consequences that ensue. Thus, while we have heard of stupid haste in war, we have not yet seen a clever operation that was prolonged[8]. There has never been a case in which a prolonged war has benefited a country[9]. Therefore, only those who understand the dangers inherent in employing troops know how to conduct war in the most profitable way.

Those adept in employing troops do not require a second levy of conscripts[10] or more than two provisionings[11]. They carry military supplies from the homeland and make up for their provisions relying on the enemy[12]. Thus the army will be always plentifully provided.

When a country is impoverished by military operations, it is because an army far from its homeland needs a distant transportation. Being forced to carry supplies for great distances renders the people destitute. On the other hand, the local price of commodities normally rises high in the area near the military camps. The rising prices cause financial resources to be drained away. When the resources are exhausted, the peasantry will be afflicted with urgent exactions[13]. With this depletion of strength and exhaustion of wealth, every household in the homeland is left empty[14]. Seven-tenths of the people's income is dissipated and six-tenths of the government's revenue is paid for broken-down chariots, worn-out horses, armor and helmets, arrows and crossbows, halberds and bucklers, spears and body shields, draught oxen and heavy wagons[15].

Hence a wise general is sure of getting provisions from the enemy countries. One jar of grains obtained from local area is equal to twenty jars shipped from the home country; one dan (60kg) of fodder[16] in the conquered area is equal to twenty dan (1200kg) from the domestic store.

Now in order to kill the enemy, our men must be roused to anger; to gain enemy's property, our men must be rewarded with war trophies[17]. Accordingly, in chariot battle, when more than ten chariots have been captured, those who took the enemy chariot first should be rewarded. Then, the enemy's flags and banners should be replaced with ours; the captured chariots mixed with ours and mounted by our men. The prisoners of war should be kindly treated and kept. This is called "becoming stronger in the course of defeating the enemy".

Hence, what is valued in war is a quick victory, not prolonged operations. And therefore, the general who understands war is the controller of his people's fate[18] and the guarantor of the security of the nation[19].

2. 1 Notes

1. Swift chariots: light chariot pulled by a team of four horses

2. Heavy chariots: used to carry army provisions and instruments

3. Transportation: carry

4. Guests: state guests and diplomatic envoys

5. Materials such as glue and lacquer: adhesive paint used in the ancient times to maintain the bow, arrow, armor and shield. Here it broadens its meaning to refer to the materials used to maintain all military instruments.

6. Army engages in protracted campaigns: the army fights outside

for a long time

7. Exhausted: tired out

8. While we have heard of stupid haste in war, we have not yet seen a clever operation that was prolonged: we know that there were stupid commanders who haste for quick victory, but never know that there were clever ones who will prolong a war for victory.

9. There has never been a case in which a prolonged war has benefited a country: Du Mu noted that: " war is a lethal weapon, too much time will change it."

10. Do not require a second levy of conscripts: the Chinese in the original text means roster, now it is used as a verb here to mean register and conscript.

11. Do not require…more than two provisioning: do not carry the provisioning many times

12. Make up for their provisions relying on the enemy: take provisions from the enemies.

13. Be afflicted with urgent exactions: the Chinese in the original text is Qiuyi, meaning exactions. In ancient China, the state collected exactions by the qiu which is composed of 128 households.

14. Every household in the homeland is left empty: every household within the state become poor and empty due to the transportation of provisions to the far-away battlefield.

15. Draught oxen and heavy wagons: oxen drafted from military service and heavy wagons pulled by oxen to carry military supplies.

16. One dan (60kg) of fodder: fodder means the feed of horses and oxen. Dan is a capacity unit in ancient China, 15 kilograms is a jun, and 4 jun is one dan.

17. To gain enemy's property, our men must be rewarded with war trophies: if we want to encourage our soldiers to take away the enemy's property, we must reward them with property.

18. The controller of his people's fate: people, the populace; controller of fate, master of the people's fate.

19. The guarantor of the security of the nation: the master or controller of the security of the nation.

2.2 Explanation

Sun Tzu said: according to the general law of operating war, it needs a thousand chariots, a hundred thousand soldiers armed to the teeth, and the transportation of provisions over a thousand miles. It costs a lot of money every day to cover the expenditure of logistics and that at the frontline, the expense used to entertain guests, to maintain glue and lacquer, weapons, chariots and armors and to purchase military supplies. Only when the above things are ready can the hundred thousand soldiers set out. If the war is protracted, the army will become exhausted. If the army attacks cities regardless of the consequences, the combat effectiveness will reduce. If the army fights for a long time outside the state, the state can hardly meet the need of the expenditure on war. If a state's army is exhausted, its pep dampened, its military forces and its treasure worn out, other states will take the advantage of this to attack it. At that time, no commander, no matter how resourceful he is, can avert the disastrous consequences it may ensue. That explains why we have heard about that there are cases of stupid tactics for quick victory but cases of clever tactics for prolonging the war. Thus, those who do not completely know the dangers of prolonging the war will not fully understand the benefits of quick operation of war.

Those who are adept in operating war will neither conscript from the home country for a second time nor transport the provisions twice. They take military weapons from the homeland but seize provisions from the enemy. So the army provisions are always adequate.

The reason why a country will be impoverished due to war is that an army far from the homeland needs a distant transportation of military provisions. The distant transportation not only exhausts the financial resources but increases the taxes on people for the people's money are exhausted due to that the price in the area where the army is stationed rises. The depletion of human resources and the exhaustion of financial resources leave every household in the country empty. Seven tenths of the people's property will be dissipated and six tenths of the government's military expenditure will be paid for fixing chariots, treating military horses, replenishing armors, helmets, crossbows, arrows, equipping halberds, bucklers, spears and body shields, and supplying draught oxen and heavy wagons.

Therefore, a wise commander will make sure to take provisions from the enemy, supplying provisions to army by fighting. A jar of grains seized from the enemy is equal to twenty jars carried from its own country and a dan (60kg) of fodder obtained from the enemy is equal to twenty dan (1200kg) from homeland.

Thus in order to kill the enemy, the commander has to boost the soldiers' morale. In order to encourage the soldiers to take the enemy's property, the commander has to reward them. Thus in chariot battle, when more than ten chariots have been captured, those who took the enemy chariot first should be rewarded. Then we should replace the enemy's flags and banners with ours and use both the captured chariots and our own. We should also kindly treated the captives and respect them. This is called becoming stronger in the course of defeating the enemy. What is important in war is a quick victory rather than protracted operations. Therefore, a wise commander is the controller of the survival of his people and nation.

2.3 Analysis

"What is valued in war is a quick victory, not prolonged operations" is an important operational principle raised in this chapter. Any war is a great consumption of human resources, material resources and financial resources. The consequences of these consumptions will in the end be borne by the people, which will bring great loss to their life and property. Therefore, the long a war is, the more harmful it is to the national economy and people's livelihood. From this perspective, "what is valued in war is a quick victory, not prolonged operations."

During the War of Resistance against Japan when the enemy was strong while we were weak in strength, we should not mechanically use the strategic principle of "what is valued in war is a quick victory, not prolonged operations." In view of this situation, Chairman Mao put forward the strategy of "protracted war" which is a typical example of creatively studying and applying *The Art of War*. Despite the fact that we have consumed a huge amount of human resources and materials, Chairman Mao's *On Protracted War* is proved to be wise and great.

Principles of operating war such as "make up for their provisions relying on the enemy" and "becoming stronger in the course of defeating the enemy" put forward by Sun Tzu are extremely brilliant strategic thoughts that have been correctly applied in practice.

So war should be operated soon instead of being protracted. Our institute has made clear requirements on the construction quality and period. The construction period is explicitly stipulated in the task assignment book that those who finish the construction earlier will be rewarded and those who fail to finish the construction on time will be punished. Therefore our employees will come back to the factory to rest right after the construction is checked and accepted. They never procrastinate. This is to the benefit of cost accounting, helps the enterprise to finish the project early and reflects its emphasis on keeping promise and honoring the contract.

That is why the commander who knows how to operate war is the controller of his people's fate and the guarantor of the security of the nation.

There are many highlights in this chapter. According to Sun Tzu, war is a waste of manpower and money. He has discussed war's dependence on human resources, materials and money.

Though an outstanding military commander, he is by no means a warmonger. He is concerned about his country and people, believing that war will increase the burden on people and drain away the national financial resources. Thus he raised the strategic thought of "what is valued in war is a quick victory, not prolonged operations."

Another highlight in this chapter is the strategic thoughts of "subdue the enemy with their own resources," "kindly treat the captives," and "forage on the enemy." Only by carrying out these thoughts can the strategic goal of "what is valued in war is a quick victory, not prolonged operations" be achieved.

Sun Tzu holds that a wise general is sure of getting provisions from the enemy countries. One jar of grains obtained from local area is equal to twenty jars shipped from the home country; one kilogram of fodder in the conquered area is equal to twenty kilogram from the domestic store.

Here, Sun Tzu keeps not only economic accounts but also political accounts, for the military provisions taken from the enemy do not cost money not even to mention the pricy transportation fee. On the other hand, taking provisions from the enemy not only has made themselves stronger but also directly weakened the enemy's fighting capacity.

So Sun Tzu encouraged the soldiers to kill the enemy and take their provisions.

In order to encourage the soldiers to kill the enemy bravely, those who contribute to the victory of war will be rewarded both in spirit and material. This strategic thought plays an important role in boosting the soldiers' morale, which has become an example for all militarists to follow.

This thought of "be fair in meting out rewards and punishments" is not only extremely important for the army but also applicable to modern enterprise management. Any wise entrepreneur who wants to manage his enterprise must mobilize the initiative of his employees. While among all the measures, being fair in meting out rewards and punishments is an important means to manage enterprise. And our institutes have benefited from it. Those who have made great contributions to translating their significant innovation into great productive forces by carrying out the scientific outlook on development should be amply rewarded. Our institute rewards those who make small contribution to scientific and technological innovation with thousands of yuan, and those who make great contribution with tens of thousands of yuan.

Sun Tzu put forward in this chapter that "The prisoners of war should be kindly treated and kept. This is called 'becoming stronger in the course of defeating the enemy." This has become the principle that militarists at all times and in all over the world will observe. Especially to those commanders who fight for justice, only by doing so can they achieve victory.

Only by being kindly treated can the captives be educated, touched, separated from other enemies and finally become part of us, a way to weaken the enemy and strengthen ourselves. In the revolutionary wars in China, we have defeated the Kuomintang army's weaponry worth eight million dollars with millet plus rifles. For instance, Beijing was liberated peacefully. Without firing a shot, the enemy surrendered to us and joined us to strengthen our military force and reinforce our weaponry. There are numerous military cases like this.

2.4 Cases

Case 1

In the famous poem *Snow* to the tune of Chin Yuan Chun, Chairman Mao wrote that "And Genghis Khan, Proud Son of Heaven for a day, Knew only shooting eagles, bow outstretched." Genghis Khan is a Mongolian, a nomadic people who bear the wild nature of a conqueror and one of whose mode of existence is robbery. In Yuan Dynasty, an age of cold weapons, it suffices to defeat other nations and conquer the world with bows and quick horses. In Genghis Khan's army, everyone is a fierce horseman and good fighter. There is no "logistics unit" in his army. So there never occurs the situation like that in the other dynasties in China where provisions set out before the army. To Khan's army, they took provisions where they fought. All the conquered nations were their logistics and their inexhaustible warehouses of military supplies. Victory is the only thing their existence relies on, for only victory can ensure them things to eat, clothes to wear and houses to live in. Once they failed, they would be starved or frozen to death. Therefore, in order to survive, they fight unusually bravely. On the battlefield, to them there was nothing but forging ahead to win victory. There allowed no retreat no failure. The Mongolian with only millions of people then had almost conquered the entire Eurasia and built the Yuan Empire of unprecedented size and maintained its brutal rule for several hundred years, which is indeed a rare miracle in the history of mankind.

Their victory derives from the strategic thinking of "make up for provisions relying on the enemy" in *The Art of War*.

Case 2

Make up for provisions relying on the enemy and subdue the enemies with their own resources.

A wise commander always makes use of the enemy's weapons to destroy the enemy. During the period of Three Kingdoms, the strong Cao's army was close on the bank of the Yangtze River and the war was on the verge of breaking. In the face of such a powerful enemy, the only way out for Liu Bei and Sun Quan is to unite to resist Cao Cao. Therefore, Liu Bei sent his military adviser Zhuge Liang to Dongwu to discuss anti-Cao plans. At the military meeting, Zhou Yu asked Zhuge Liang: "what weapons are the best for the war between land and water in the face of the natural barrier of the

Yangtze River?" Zhuge Liang replied: "The best weapon to use in the war fought in the river is bow.

Zhou proceeded to say: "The army is now short of arrows. Make sure that you can make ten thousand arrows to fight against the enemy, Master."

Zhuge said in reply: "since Governor has commissioned the task commissioned to me, I will certainly finish it. But I'm afraid ten days is too long and will bungle the chance of winning the battle."

"Then how many days do you think you need to finish the task?" asked Zhou.

"Three days is enough." answered Zhuge.

Chuckling to himself, Zhou called the army secretary to write a writ, asked Zhuge to sign on it and held a banquet for Zhuge, saying: "A military pledge or order must be carried out. You will be rewarded when the task is finished."

"Today is too late to start the task. I will start making arrows tomorrow. On the third day, I will send five hundred soldiers to get the arrows by the river." answered Zhuge who left after several cups of wine.

Lu Su questioned: "Does he cheat?"

Zhou Yu said: "I did not force him. It is himself who asks for death and falls into my trap of killing two birds with one stone."

Ordered by Zhou Yu, Lu Su came to see Zhuge Liang and find out the actual situation.

In deep friendship with Zhuge Liang, Lu Su worried about the task Zhuge Liang agreed to finish.

Seeing Lu Su, Zhuge Liang was overjoyed: "Please help me with arrow making."

"It is you yourself who had made the military pledge, how can I help you?" said Lu Su.

Zhuge Liang replied: "I hope that you can borrow me twenty boats with

37

thirty soldiers on each. Each boat should be covered with green cloth with a thousand scarecrows on both sides. But please do not let Zhou Yu know that. Otherwise my plan will fall through."

Though saying yes to Zhuge Liang, Lu Su did not understand what Zhuge Liang meant to do. But he did not mention Zhu's borrowing of boats when reporting to Zhou Yu, only saying that Zhuge Liang must have his own reason not to make arrows with arrow bamboo, feather, glue and lacquer. There arose a big doubt in Zhou Yu: "I will wait and see how you will honor the military pledge!"

Lu Su had prepared all the boats, scarecrows and cloth as required by Zhuge Liang. At about 1:00 a.m. on the third day, Zhuge Liang prepared a banquet on the boat and secretly invited Lu Su over to drink with him. With all the twenty boats tied by rope, Zhuge Liang ordered the boats to set off towards the north bank.

That night, the fog was all over the sky and even denser above the river where nothing could be seen beyond several feet. Zhuge Liang ordered the boats to march forward and stopped at Cao Cao's naval base, lining up in a row with the stem towards the west and the stern towards the east. Then he ordered the soldiers to beat the military drums and shot.

Lu Su was shocked and asked: "what can we do if Cao Cao sends out all his soldiers?"

Zhuge Liang answered, smiling: "The dense fog has enshrouded the river. Not knowing what was going on here, Cao Cao will not send the army. The only thing we need to do is sit here drink and have fun. And we are going back when the fog dispersed. "

At Cao's naval base, hearing the drum, Mao Jie and Yu Jin were fluttered and lost no time in reporting it to Cao Cao.

Cao Cao gave the order that there must be an ambush from the enemy for the fog was all over the river. Do not act rashly. Send the naval crossbowmen to shoot at the enemy. Besides, he sent Zhang Liao and Xu Huang to hurry to the bank of river each with three thousand soldiers to fiercely shoot at the enemy by following the trace of drum. About seven and eight tenths of the arrows were shot on the scarecrows. When the scarecrows on one side of each boat were crowded with arrows, Zhuge Liang ordered to turn the boat around and march towards the naval base so that the scarecrows on the other side of the boat can receive arrows. When the scarecrows on both sides of the boats were full of arrows and the fog above the river began to disperse, Zhuge Liang ordered the soldiers to drive the boats back home. The light boats were soon driven to the middle of the river by the strong torrent. It was

too late to chase the boats. Seeing that the scarecrows were full of arrows, Cao Cao was in deep regret.

Zhuge Liang finished the task on time. When Lu Su reported to Zhou Yu the process of borrowing arrows from Cao Cao, though both surprised and angry, Zhou Yu could not help exclaiming: "I am no match for Zhuge Liang for he has wonderful foresight."

By borrowing the enemy's weapons at the eve of war to destroy the enemy is called "subdue the enemies with their own resources."

In the War of Liberation, the Liberation Army seized Chiang Kai-shek's American weapons to arm themselves and make themselves stronger, which is the best example of "make up for provisions relying on the enemy" and "subdue the enemies with their own resources."

Case 3

"Mengniu" is an up-rising star in dairy groups. Its President Niu Gensheng was a close comrade-in-arms of the President of Erie before he set up Mengniu. They worked together to found the largest dairy group in China with a fixed asset of billions of yuan---Erie Group.

In business, there is no eternal "friends" but eternal interest. Just like one nation can't have two queens, they parted away due to different interests and personalities.

Niu Gensheng set up Mengniu Group after leaving Erie Group. At the initial stage of the business, Mengniu was short of both talents and capital. Compared with the dairy tycoon Erie Group, Mengniu was far from being its match. As Erie the elephant stomps, Mengniu the ant will be trampled to death.

However, Mengniu also has its own advantage, i.e. its President Niu Gensheng was professional, open-minded in solving problems and knew the dialectic relations between spending money and earning money and was good at discovering able people and putting them at suitable posts. All the technical backbones and middle-level managers from Erie will be put in an important position, promoted and given salary increase. At that time in Hohhot, the salary in Mengniu Group is the highest. Its middle managers can earn a hundred thousand yuan a year. No matter what difficulties he had met in finance, he had never treated unfairly the "captives" coming from his opponent. He has staunchly followed the policy of "treating the captives well" and the strategic guideline of "make up for provisions relying on the enemy" in *The Art of War*. He has realized that in today's business war, all competitions with the opponents, in the final analysis, are the competition for talents. In a very short time, he has attracted three to four hundred professional from Erie Dairy Group. He has fulfilled his great cause of Mengniu at the minimal cost, making Mengniu overtake Erie in all aspects and become the largest dairy group through its ten years of efforts from 1999 to 2009.

If we summarize the reason why Mengniu can overtake Erie from the perspective of *The Art of War*, its experience of success are the following:

1. Niu Gensheng used to work in Erie and thus made it to know the enemy and know himself.

2. Niu Gensheng was generous to people and made it to kindly treat the captives and thus dissipate their worries and make them focus on their work.

3. Niu Gensheng made it to "make up for provisions relying on the enemy" for he has realized the importance of talents and was good at discovering able people and putting them at suitable posts.

Case 4

Sun Tzu said: "what is valued in war is a quick victory, not prolonged operations. And therefore, the general who understands war is the controller of his people's fate and the guarantor of the security of the nation.

Dalian Katelin Specific Alloy Institute has benefited a lot by carrying out the operational principle of "what is valued in war is a quick victory, not prolonged operations." When our institute was flame plating for large power plants, there were many rushed urgent and heavy tasks. If we failed to finish each task on time, the production plan of the power plant would be influenced and we would suffer economic punishment which is a lot of money. Besides, our employees who went for a first-aid repair have to live in hotel. And if the hotel is far away, they even have to hail a taxi to work and they eat outside for all three meals. All of these cost a lot. Therefore, we require our employees to finish the job outside quickly, which can help to finish the task of the power plant in advance and save the expenses of the institute. So our opinion is that "what is valued in a project is speed."

1. Use advanced equipment. We used the innovative supersonic broad arc spraying machine invented by our institute. Its high production efficiency is vital to finishing the task in advance.

2. Practice three shifts to finish the task as soon as possible.

3. Carry forward the spirit of working hard and the style of being good at fighting tough. We receive compliments from our clients for we finish the task on time every time. This has set up a good image of our institute and our employees have been praised by power plants many times. The supersonic broad arc spraying machine and the high-strength wear resistant alloy invented by ourselves is welcome by all power plants for the high quality and speed of the construction. And they have won the third-class award of scientific and technological invention awarded by Dalian Municipal People's Government.

Life should be boiling rather than mediocre and inactive. And scientific research is just designed to serve productivity.

-Author's note

Chapter 3
ATTACK BY STRATAGEM

Sun Tzu believed that the best policy in war is to subdue the enemy is to use strategies rather than fight. In this way, not only the casualties in war can be reduced but also the destruction of economy can be avoided.

He also raised the axiom that "if you know your enemies and know yourself, you can win a hundred battles without a single loss." It is a military classic of great wisdom of dialectical materialism.

Sun Tzu said: Generally in war the best thing of all is to take the enemy's state whole and intact[1], to ruin it[2] is inferior to this. To capture the enemy's army[3] entire is better than to destroy it; to take intact a battalion, a company or a five-man squad is better than to destroy them. Hence to win a hundred victories in one hundred battles is not the acme of skill. To subdue the enemy without fighting is the supreme excellence.

Thus, the best policy in war is to attack the enemy's strategy[4]. The second best way is to disrupt his alliances through diplomatic means[5]. The next best method is to attack his army in the field. The worst policy is to attack walled cities. Attacking cities is the last resort when there is no alternative. It takes at least three months to make mantlets and shielded vehicles[6] ready and prepare necessary arms and equipment. It takes at least another three months to pile up earthen mounds[7] over against the walls. The general unable to control his impatience will order his troops to swarm up the wall like ants[8] with the result that one third of them are slain, while the cities remain untaken[9]. Such is the calamity of attacking walled cities.

Therefore, those skilled in war subdue the enemy's army without fighting[10]. They capture the enemy's cities without assaulting them and overthrow his state without protracted operations[11]. Their aim must be to take all under heaven intact through strategic superiority. Thus, their troops are not worn out[12] and their triumph will be complete. This is the art of attacking by stratagem[13].

Consequently, the art of using troops is this: When ten to the enemy's one[14], surround him. When five times his strength, attack him. If double his strength, divide him. If equally matched, engage him[15]. If less in number, be capable of defending yourself[16]. And if in all respects unfavorable, be capable of eluding him. Hence, a weak force will eventually fall captive to a strong one if it is simply holds ground and conducts a desperate defense[17].

Now, the general is the bulwark of the state: if the bulwark is complete at all points[18], the state will surely be strong; if the bulwark is defective[19], the state will certainly be weak.

Now, there are three ways in which a sovereign can bring misfortune upon his army: 1) By ordering an advance while ignorant of the fact that the army cannot go forward, or by ordering[20] a retreat while ignorant of the fact that the army cannot fall back. This is described as "hobbling the army"[21]. 2) By interfering with[22] the army's administration without knowledge of the internal affairs of the army. This causes officers and soldiers to be perplexed. 3) By interfering with direction of fighting, while ignorant of the military principle of adaptation to circumstances. This sows doubts and misgivings in the minds of his officers and soldiers. If the army is confused and suspicious, neighboring rulers will take advantage of this and cause trouble. This is simply bringing anarchy into the army and flinging victory away[23].

Thus, there are five points in which victory may be predicted[24]: he who knows when to fight and when not to fight will win; he who understands how to handle both superior and inferior forces will win; he whose ranks are united in purpose will win; he who is well prepared and lies in wait for an enemy who is not well prepared[25] will win; he whose generals are able and not interfered with by the sovereign will win. It is in these five points that the way to victory is known.

Therefore, I say: Know the enemy and know yourself, and you can fight a hundred battles with no danger of defeat[26]. When you are ignorant of the enemy but know yourself, your chances of winning and losing are equal. If ignorant both of your enemy and of yourself, you are sure to be defeated in every battle.

3.1 Notes

1. Take the enemy's state whole and intact: subdue the enemy without a fight.

2. Ruin it: defeat the enemy's state with military force.

3. Army: it, together with battalion, company, squad, is a military unit in ancient time in China. An army consists of 12,500 men, a battalion of 500, a company of 100 and a squad of 5.

4. The best policy in war is to attack the enemy's strategy: it is best to win the war by using strategies.

5. Disrupt his alliances through diplomatic means: to defeat the enemy by diplomacy.

6. Make mantlets and shielded vehicles: make, build. mantlet: a large shield made of rattan; shielded vehicles: a wooden four-wheeler covered with rawhide used to haul earth to fill the moat and attack the city in ancient time. It is can hold a dozen of men.

7. Pile up earthen mounds: build earthen mounds to climb over the wall to attack the enemy.

8. Order his troops to swarm up the wall like ants: order the troops to climb the city wall like ants.

9. Untaken: not captured.

10. Without fighting: to subdue the enemy with strategies and diplomacy

11. Overthrow his state without protracted operations: destroy the enemy's state not by long time war.

12. Their troops are not worn out: their fighting capacity and morale do not decrease.

13. Attacking by stratagem: attack the enemy with strategies.

14. When ten to the enemy's one: when our strength is about ten times that of the enemy. Here ten times is not necessarily ten times, it only means we have absolute advantages compared with the enemy.

15. If double his strength, divide him. If equally matched, engage him: when your strength is twice that of your enemy, you can divide them and destroy them. And if you are equal with your enemy in strength, you can beat them back.

16. Defending yourself: try not to confront your enemy.

17. A weak force will eventually fall captive to a strong one if it is simply holds ground and conducts a desperate defense: though a weak force will fight obstinately, in the end it will be captured by the stronger one.

18. If the bulwark is complete at all points: complete in wits to assist the state.

19. If the bulwark is defective: have weakness in assisting the state.

20. Ordering: giving order to.

21. Hobbling the army: fettering the army.

22. Interfering with: meddling

23. Bringing anarchy into the army and flinging victory away: the confusion in our army will lead to the success of the enemy.

24. Victory may be predicted: victory can be forecast

25. Well prepared: be ready for

26. Defeat: loss

3.2 Explanation

Sun Tzu said that according to the general law of conducting a war, the best policy is to capture the enemy's state whole and intact while to destroy it with military force is inferior to the former policy. It is better to capture the enemy's entire than to destroy it, to make the entire battalion, company or squad yield than to destroy them. Thus, though to win a hundred victories in a hundred battles is excellent, it is not supreme excellence. The supreme excellence consists in subduing the enemy without fighting.

Therefore, the best policy of using military forces is to attack the enemy with strategies. The second best is to defeat the enemy with diplomacy. And the next best policy is to win the battle with military forces, while attacking the enemy's walled city is the last resort, for it takes several months to make mantlets and large chariots and prepare all kinds of equipment for attacking the enemy's city, and another few months is needed to pile up the small earthen mounds for the attack. Then, the general could hardly suppress his own anger and order the soldiers to swarm up the scaling ladder like ants, which will possibly cause one third of them die while the enemy's city remains untaken. Such is the calamity brought by attacking the walled city. Hence, he who is adept in conducting war always subdues enemy's army rather than takes the enemy's moat by fighting and overthrows the enemy's state without protracted fighting. His aim is to take all under heaven intact with complete victory. In this way, his army can win a sweeping victory without being worn out. Such is the basic principle of winning victories by stratagem.

Therefore, the art of using troops is: when our armed forces is ten times that of the enemy, besiege him; when five times, launch a fierce attack against him; when double, divide him; when equally matched, resist and confront them; when less in number, try to defend ourselves; when we are inferior to the enemy in military strength, try to avoid fighting them as much as possible, for the weaker force, not matter how desperately they fight, will in the end be captured by the stronger one.

The commander is the pillar of the state. If he is thoughtful in assisting the monarch, the state will be strong, while if he is careless in that, the state will be weak.

There are three ways in which the monarch will bring disaster to military operations: ordering the army to attack while it cannot attack and commanding the army to retreat while it cannot retreat, which is called "fettering the army;" interfering with military management knowing nothing about it, which perplexes the commanders and the soldiers; meddling in military conduction while ignorant of the change of strategies in military operations, which generate doubts in the commanders and the soldiers. If the entire army is confused and suspicious, the neighboring states will take advantage of this to attack us and disaster will ensue. This is called defeating yourself and presenting the enemy with the chance of making use of our self-defeat to win the victory.

Thus, there are five essentials victory: he who knows clearly when to fight and when not to fight will win; he who knows what strategies to adopt according to his armed forces will win; he whose soldiers fight with him of one heart and one mind for the same goal will win; he who is well prepared and waits to attack the enemy that is unprepared will win; he who is gifted and not fettered by the monarch will win. These are the ways to predict victory.

Hence, if you know the enemy and know yourself, you can win a hundred battles without a single loss. If you know yourself but the enemy, your chances of winning and losing are equal. If you know neither your enemy nor yourself, you will be defeated in every battle.

3.3 Analysis

The highlights in this chapter are as follows:

1. The best policy in war is to attack the enemy's strategy.

2. The relationship between the monarch and the commander who conducts the war outside should be set right.

3. Know the enemy and know yourself, and you can fight a hundred battles with no danger of defeat.

First of all, this chapter puts forward that the best policy in war is to attack the enemy's strategy, which is the core of *The Art of War*. "The best policy in war is to attack the enemy's strategy[4]. The second best way is to disrupt his alliances through diplomatic means[5]. The next best method is to attack his army in the field. The worst policy is to attack walled cities." These words have shown us the important military thought of winning the victory with wits. Sun Tzu deems the great wisdom and strategies as the best means of winning victories. He advocates win by stratagem rather than by brutal fighting. And clearly such a general is the best commander of war.

Secondly, Sun Tzu believes that though the supreme ruler of a state, the sovereign must respect the highest generals of military on the front line, for they are the direct commanders who are right on the front line and who knows the process of war the best. If the sovereign, knowing nothing of the situation of the war, interferes with the conduction of war with his rights, he will surely influence the normal command of the army and cause defeat in the battle.

"Know the enemy and know yourself, and you can fight a hundred battles with no danger of defeat." This is a military classic of great wisdom in dialectics. By "know the enemy and know yourself," Sun Tzu does not mean simply know the enemy's situation. He also means that the way to predict a victory is by analyzing and judging the opportunity for combat, the number of soldiers, the will of the people, the unity, the preparation, the weather, the geographical location, the support of the people, the general's command capability, talents and his choice of people, etc.

3.4 Cases

Case 1

Sun Tzu said: "Know the enemy and know yourself, and you can fight a hundred battles with no danger of defeat[26]. When you are ignorant of the enemy but know yourself, your chances of winning and losing are equal. If ignorant both of your enemy and of yourself, you are sure to be defeated in every battle." Following this principle, our institute has avoided taking many detours and achieved unexpected results.

We believe that enterprise management and business war are the same with war, for victory can be won only by knowing the enemy and yourself in these fields.

Take scientific research as an example, we have to fully understand the object of our research. As the object of our research is metal surface, we need to have a deep and careful understanding of the operating environment and feature of metal surface under different working conditions, such as high-temperature wear resistance, shock wear resistance and fatigue wear resistance. In high temperature, the metal surface of the water wall tube of the boiler used to generate electricity is subject to strong friction caused by the floating up and down of the coal bed. Therefore, the metal surface is easy to be frayed and leak and thus cause great damage to electricity generation and heating in winter. This is what we call "know the enemy." In order to solve the problem of wear resistance of metal in high temperature, we must choose quality metal of thermo-stability and wear resistance specific to the boiler's feature of anti-wear. So we have to "know ourselves". Can our technologies and materials meet the standards of high-temperature wear resistance? If not, we have to conduct further research and prepare new materials till they meet the requirements. This is what we call "know yourself" in scientific research. The reason why our patent in high-temperature wear resistance <ZL.011028.69.6> can meet the requirements of the boiler for generating electricity is that we have come to know the enemy and ourselves through trial and error. Similarly in enterprise management, we must know our staff's quality, specialty and in business war, we must know the rival's specialty. Only in this way can we remain invincible. From the military war between countries in a football competition,

49

we have to follow the principles *In the Art of War* to know the enemy and ourselves and finally achieve great results.

Case 2

The core of *The Art of War* is to win the victory by stratagem. In enterprise management and market competition, *The Art of War* is a must-read classic to entrepreneurs and businessmen and is listed a compulsory course of business administration. In market economy, many laws of competition communicate with those in war. "Military war" in the battlefield and "business war" in the market are both life-and-death struggle. In business war, the one who can earn more trust from the customers and whose commodities are good and cheap can win.

I.   Know the enemy and know yourself, and you can fight a hundred battles with no danger of defeat

In order to win over more customers, we have to know more about the customers: what do the consumers want? What are the local custom, the conditions of the people and the tradition of consumption? What kind of products might be welcomed? In what aspects should the products be improved to be better received? And according to the answers to these questions, we come to determine what new opportunities the enterprise should seize and what innovations the enterprise should make.

If we want to put our products into the international market and integrate with the international economy, we have to be familiar with the international laws and regulations, international finance, intellectual property protection, anti-dumping, environmental protection and other issues. We have to be both law-abiding and be good at using legal knowledge to protect ourselves.

As people's lives continue to improve, we must be quick to tap the customers' potential consumption power, open new market and seize the initiative in enterprise competition. To know your enemy is extremely important in enterprise and business management.

We should make a right assessment of our strength according to the demand of market and find out what our advantages and disadvantages are so that we can use our limited resources where we can make the best use of them.

In market competition, we have to find out who are our real rivals and know

50

everything about them as know about ourselves. What their strengths and weaknesses are. We have to be good at attack others' weaknesses with our strengths. To make strategies according to the enemy's situation is called "know the enemy."

As the global economies integrate, our rivals are not only bounded within the country. They are scattered all over the world. An enterprise should measure its own standard against the goal made and realized by all the most advanced enterprises in the same industry all over the world so that it can know its status quo, find the gap between the highest standard and itself and set the highest standard as its strategic goal.

The fact that he international and national markets are always in flux is determined by politics, economy, technology, finance, culture and management. There is a time gap between the two markets when the changes are reflected in them. To seize these changes is of great benefit to the enterprise to take the right strategies and move faster to seize the business opportunity to develop itself.

II. He who knows when to fight and when not to fight will win.

There are five points in which victory may be predicted: he who knows when to fight and when not to fight will win; he who understands how to handle both superior and inferior forces will win; he whose ranks are united in purpose will win; he who is well prepared and lies in wait for an enemy who is not well prepared will win; he whose generals are able and not interfered with by the sovereign will win. It is in these five points that the way to victory is known.

In market economy, any industry and its products and service are providing new business opportunity to enterprises. Some enterprises develop from the operation of one product to that of different products in different industries. Spreading risk can provide the enterprise with the opportunity to make profits and develop. There are also some overconfident enterprises that are reduced to bankruptcy due to engaging in too many different industries. One thing for sure is that an enterprise, on its way to development, should not break away from its original advantages. It should extend on the basis of these advantages rather than in a blind way. If the enterprise only sees the profitable opportunities in the market and expands rashly without making a sober analysis of its own ability of mastering it, it contains in itself a huge risk. This is just an important support of the Sun Tzu's opinion that he who knows when to fight and when not to fight will win.

III. Differentiate rivals and avoid vicious competition.

Each of the two contradictory aspects can transform itself into the other. Some rivals are not enemies but friends. Some rivals helps to realize our strategic goal, strengthen the enterprise's enduring competitive advantages and improve the structure of the industry.

The strength of an enterprise is limited. If an enterprise treats all rivals as objects of attack without analyzing them, it will not only feel unable to do so but also destroy its own competitive advantages. On the contrary, if an enterprise selectively competes with certain rivals, it can focus its advantages to strike down the rivals one by one.

An enterprise should try not to confront its rivals and to avoid excessive competition and thus win the victory.

Nowadays, more and more enterprises have benefited from cooperation. Thus they have established the guild and set up strategic alliance to help each other in technology, information and resources.

IV. Take the initiative and "imposes his will on the enemy, but does not allow the enemy's will to be imposed on him."

The market is made up of customers. As the economy develops and people's living standards continue to improve, the demands of customers tend to be more and more diversified. Thus, there are huge potential demands to be tapped. If you only see the actual market, your rivals are already one step ahead of you to go to the battlefield. Even if you finally force a way in, it is too late for you are already put in unfavorable position. Therefore, we have to impose our will on the enemy but not allow their will to be imposed on us so that we can take the initiative in market competition.

The enterprise must make a careful investigation and analysis in the first place to choose its targeted customers. Focusing on this potential demands, the enterprise should consider for the customers and see things from the customers' perspectives. By turning the potential demands of the customers into real one and turning the potential customers into real customers, the enterprise has successfully turned the potential market into actual market. All enterprises must rely on markets, go to the hearts of the customers and raise the potential hope, wish and desire of the customers as the new subjects so that they can think about them carefully and   analyze them to build new ways of operating, which is the inspiration and source of making innovations in products and opening new markets. For instance, the disposable dinner box, after being used, will produce a huge amount of rubbish. So can we make the disposable dinner box into some tasty food and eat it after eating the meal? Based on this idea, the study of what materials can be made into edible dinner box that can hold meal and taste pleasant so that it can be eaten after the meal is conducted. After a careful study, such a type of dinner box was finally invented and well received at its first appearance in China and Japan. A small dinner box has brought a big fortune. It has helped people to realize the dream of becoming rich. Only by continuous innovation can an enterprise set up its own unique market and ensure its success in market competition.

Case 3

Sun Tzu said: "Therefore, those skilled in war subdue the enemy's army without fighting. They capture the enemy's cities without assaulting them and overthrow his state without protracted operations. Their aim must be to take all under heaven intact through strategic superiority. Thus, their troops are not worn out and their triumph will be complete. This is the art of attacking by stratagem."

Here, Sun Tzu has attached great importance to winning by stratagem. In fact, after studying *The Art of War*, our institute believes that winning by stratagem is the core of the strategies in the book and its living soul. In order to inherit the precious cultural heritage from our ancestors, we have to inherit their tremendous courage and wisdom. The scientific outlook on development put forward by President Hu Jiantao is a great theory full of wisdom. It is an ideological weapon that calls on us to winning with wisdom, reviving the country with wits and developing the country with strategies. According to the strategic thought of winning by stratagem in *The Art of War* and combining the scientific outlook on development raised by President Hu Jintao, our institute has made a comprehensive summary of the achievements we have made under the guidance of the scientific outlook on development since it was set up, and wrote the paper *Practicing Scientific Outlook on Development is the Inexhaustible Source of Development of Productive Forces*, which was awarded by the Chinese Academy of Management Science the First Prize of Excellent Paper.

It is written in the paper that through scientific and technological progress, productive forces have developed from "the productive forces of man power" and "the productive forces of machines" to "the productive forces of culture" with highly advanced science and technology. In this long and arduous struggle, human beings have created the history and the advanced civilization of the development of productive forces. To satisfy the continuously growing material demands of human, technological innovations are needed to improve people's livelihood. People have to adopt more advanced technologies to carry out production activities and thus raise the productive forces to a new level. The productive forces develop like this step by step. The paper has put forth the following arguments: first, the core of the scientific outlook on development is people first; secondly, the decision of the scientific outlook on development is reform and opening up; thirdly, the soul of the scientific outlook on development is independent innovation; fourthly, the first prerequisite of the scientific outlook on development is development; fifthly, the guiding principle of the scientific outlook on development is comprehensive, coordinate and sustainable development.

Through the above five arguments, the paper has made a comprehensive summary of the substantial achievements the institute has made under the guidance of the scientific outlook on development and come to the conclusion that practicing the scientific outlook on development is the inexhaustible source of the development of productive forces. The essence of winning by stratagem is to make constant innovation according to the law of the scientific outlook on development.

Those who can make great achievements, create scientific miracles and become great scientists are all "forced" to be that way.

-Author's note

On the road of innovation, one should be brave to climb the peaks of science, take the twisting road and be ready to cross the gate of hell."

-Author's note

Chapter 4
DISPOSITION OF MILITARY STRENGTH

The Militarist adept in war always create conditions to put his forces in an invincible position and at the same time miss no opportunity to defeat the enemy. Therefore, a triumphant army will not fight with the enemy until they have created conditions for victory. In this way, it is in his power to control the success of the war.

Sun Tzu said: The skillful warriors in ancient times first made themselves invincible[1] and then awaited the enemy's moment of vulnerability[2]. Invincibility depends on oneself, but the enemy's vulnerability on himself[3]. It follows that those skilled in war can make themselves invincible but cannot cause an enemy to be certainly vulnerable. Therefore, it can be said that, one may know how to achieve victory, but cannot necessarily do so[4]. Defend yourself when the enemy's strength is abundant[5]; and attack the enemy when it is inadequate. Standing on the defensive indicates insufficient strength; attacking, a superabundance of strength[6]. Those who are skilled in defense hide themselves as under the most secret recesses of earth[7]; those skilled in attack flash forth as from above the topmost heights of heaven[8]. Thus, they are capable both of protecting themselves and of gaining a complete victory.

To foresee a victory no better than ordinary people's foresight is not the acme of excellence. Neither is it the acme of excellence if you win a victory through fierce fighting and the whole empire says, "Well done!"[9] Hence, by analogy, to lift a hair[10] does not signify great strength; to see the sun and moon does not signify good sight; to hear the thunderclap does not signify acute hearing[11]. In ancient times, those called skilled in war conquered an enemy easily conquered[12]. Consequently, a master of war wins victories without showing his brilliant military success, and without gaining the reputation for wisdom or the merit for valor[13]. He wins his victories without making mistakes[14]. Making no mistakes is what establishes the certainty of victory, for it means that he conquers an enemy already defeated. Accordingly, a wise commander always ensures that his forces are put in an invincible position, and at the same time will be sure to miss no opportunity to defeat the enemy[15]. It follows that a triumphant army will not fight with the enemy until the victory is assured[16], while an army destined to defeat will always fight with his opponent first, in the hope that it may win by sheer good luck[17]. The commander adept in war enhances the moral influence and adheres to the laws and regulations. Thus it is in his power[18] to control success.

Now, the elements of the art of war are first, the measurement of space; second, the estimation of quantities; third, the calculation of figures; fourth, comparisons of strength and fifth, chances of victory. Measurements of space are derived from the ground. Quantities derive from measurement, figures from quantities, comparisons from figures, and victory from comparisons.

Therefore, a victorious army is as one dollar balanced against a cent, and a defeated army is as a cent balanced against one dollar.

An army superior in strength takes action like the bursting of pent-up waters into a chasm of a thousand fathoms deep. This is what the disposition of military strength means in the actions of war.

4.1 Notes

1. First made themselves invincible: put themselves in the invincible position.

2. Awaited the enemy's moment of vulnerability: waited for the opportunity of defeating the enemy

3. Invincibility depends on oneself, but the enemy's vulnerability on himself: one needs to make efforts to create the conditions of not being defeated by the enemy. While whether the enemy can be defeated depends on whether the enemy makes mistakes. It is not what we can decide.

4. One may know how to achieve victory, but cannot necessarily do so: the victory can be predicted but we cannot decide whether the enemy has the opportunity to defeat us.

5. Defend yourself when the enemy's strength is abundant: if you are not sure of winning the war, defend yourself.

6. Standing on the defensive indicates insufficient strength; attacking, a superabundance of strength: when defending yourself, it is because you are in an unfavorable situation. When attacking, it is because your forces gain the upper hand.

7. Hide themselves as under the most secret recesses of earth: hide themselves secretly.

8. Flash forth as from above the topmost heights of heaven: the attack is so powerful as a thunderbolt that the enemy cannot withstand.

9. Neither is it the acme of excellence if you win a victory through fierce fighting and the whole empire says, "Well done": if you win a war by fighting hard and people all praise high of it, it is not the best of all.

10. A hair: the hair of birds and beasts when they molt, it means extremely light and can be lifted with no effort.

11. To hear the thunderclap does not signify acute hearing: even if you can hear a thunderclap, it does not mean that you have keen hearing.

12. Those called skilled in war conquered an enemy easily conquered: those who adept in war seem to defeat the enemy with no effort.

13. without showing his brilliant military success, and without gaining the reputation for wisdom or the merit for valor: the people do not know that he (a master of war) can predict a victory and thus he does not win the reputation for wisdom; the enemies surrendered before being killed, so he do not gain the merit for valor.

14. Mistake: error.

15. Miss no opportunity to defeat the enemy: do not miss any opportunity to defeat the enemy.

16. A triumphant army will not fight with the enemy until the victory is assured: the armies that can win always create conditions for victory before fighting the enemy.

17. An army destined to defeat will always fight with his opponent first, in the hope that it may win by sheer good luck: the army that is defeated always fight with the enemy rashly, hoping that they can win by good luck.

18. Power: ability

4.2 Explanation

Sun Tzu said: the past militarists skilled in operating war always first created favorable conditions not to be defeated by the enemy and waited for the opportunity to defeat the enemy. It is completely by one's own effort not to be defeated by the enemy, yet whether the enemy can be defeated depends on whether the enemy gives us the opportunity to defeat him. Thus, though being able to not be defeated by the enemy, those good at commanding troops cannot ensure the victory. That's why we say that victory can be predicted but cannot be won by mere subjective wishes.

When you cannot defeat the enemy, you should focus on strategic defense. When you are able to defeat the enemy, you should give first place to strategic attack. To stand on the defensive is because that the enemy is stronger than us. To attack is because that the enemy is weaker than us. The army adept in defending can hide under the most secret recesses and no one can find a trace of it. And the army good at attacking charges as from above the topmost heights of heaven, the power of which cannot be resisted. Hence, an army skilled in both defending and attacking is able to both protecting themselves and destroying the enemy.

To predict a victory no better than ordinary people is not the best illustration of excellence. The victory praised by everyone is not the best either. This is just like the one that can lift a hair does not necessarily have great strength, the one who can see the sun and the moon does not necessarily have good eyesight and the one who can hear the thunderclap does not necessarily have good hearing. Those who are said to be good at war in ancient times always defeated the enemy who was easily to be defeated. Therefore, a real master of war wins victories without showing his wisdom and gaining the reputation of valor. The reason why they can win victories is that they make no mistake in the operation of war. While their success in making no mistake is due to the fact that the strategies they used in the war is based on the certainty of victory. Conducting the war in this way is as if fighting with the enemy that has already been defeated. A master of war invariably creates conditions to put himself in an invincible position first and then miss no opportunity to defeat the enemy. Hence, a triumphant army will not fight the enemy until it has created the conditions for victory, while a defeated army always fights the enemy first, in the hope that it may win victories by sheer good luck. Only by adhering to military regulations can a master of war holds in his hand the initiative to control the outcome of the war.

There are five categories in the art of military; the first one is the size of the homeland of the two countries engaged in war; second, the number of their population and soldiers; third, the amount of their properties and resources; fourth, the comparison of their military strength; and the fifth, their advantages and disadvantages and the way to win victories. As both of the two countries have homeland, the measurement of space comes into being; their difference in the measurement of space gives rise to the quantities of their strategic supplies; their difference in the quantities of strategic supplies produces the number of soldiers; their difference in the number of soldiers generates the comparison of their military strength which finally decides the outcome of the war.

Thus, the way a triumphant army fights is as one dollar balanced against a cent, and a defeated army fights as a cent balanced against one dollar. A victorious army fights like the water bursting into a chasm of a thousand fathoms deep, which is as powerful as a thunderbolt that cannot be resisted.

4.3 Analysis

The "disposition" in this chapter is closely related to the "energy" in chapter five and they have something in common. "Energy" means two things: military strength and the comparison between the two. The "energy" in its dynamic existence is a both visible and invisible strategic thought in which men's subjective initiative is consistent with the objective reality and that can influence the outcome of war. Those who are skilled in war defeat the enemy that can be easily defeated rather than the one that is hard to defeat. "In ancient times, those called skilled in war conquered an enemy easily conquered." This is an original dialectical thought.

The victories won by the commander adept in winning victories are often ordinary. The secret of the certainty of such ordinary victories lies in the pre-war preparation. If you create the favorable conditions, you can turn the favorable conditions in each battle into conditions of victory. Therefore, "making no mistakes is what establishes the certainty of victory, for it means that he conquers an enemy already defeated."

4.4 Cases

Case 1

An excellent businessman, in enterprise management, always gives top priority to training the quality of his staff which includes political caliber and professional quality. As the saying goes that armies are to be maintained in the course of long years, but to be used in the nick of time, maintaining armies is training soldiers. The more training they get, the better they become and the more straight they can shoot. Only the best picked troops can win victories in war.

The staff in our institute usually gets training before going to take the position. All the workers on the production line must have a work license. They have to receive training on systems, safety, operations and best practices. The work license is only given when they have passed the test and successfully operated on the frontline of production. We do this completely out of being responsible for our customers.

Practice makes perfect. There are slow seasons and busy seasons in our institute. In slow seasons when there are few tasks, we spend most of the time training our staff. In the process of training, we hold a competition to see who is the most skillful and who operates according to standards and thus choose the model technician. As this even is related to the income of the staff, everyone studies and works hard.

The superior quality of our staff has ensured the quality of our service and thus guaranteed the popularity among our customers.

The strategic thought of "first creating the conditions to be put in an invincible position" in enterprise management is reflected in the strict requirement on each employee. Only by being well trained can the employees ensure good quality in work.

Sun Tzu said: "The skillful warriors in ancient times first made themselves invincible and then awaited the enemy's moment of vulnerability. Invincibility depends on oneself, but the enemy's vulnerability on himself." Only by making full preparation and training to be better in technology can we put ourselves in an invincible position and then wait for the opportunity to defeat the enemy. The key to being not to be defeated lie in that we should create enough conditions. And whether we can defeat the enemy depends on whether there occurs in their camps the opportunity that can be exploited to our advantage. As long as we seize the opportunity, we can destroy them totally.

"Accordingly, a wise commander always ensures that his forces are put in an invincible position, and at the same time will be sure to miss no opportunity to defeat the enemy." *The Art of War* has repeatedly emphasized "being put in an invincible position." It is the very brilliant thing about enterprise management. There is a saying that poverty is eating irrelevant, dressing irrelevant, but calculations are critical. In the art of war, it can be put in this way: failure means attack is irrelevant but planning is critical. It is not too hard to operate the troops in war and be victorious as long as you are ready for war at all time.

It is the same with enterprise management. In order to "first make ourselves invincible," we have to have the funds and management in place, to avoid the disturbances brought by economic crisis, build an efficient management team, set up modern enterprise system, improve the operation capability, mobilize the staff's enthusiasm and pool the wisdom and efforts of everyone, so that we can perform well in all work.

Enterprise operation should be based on the thought of "first make ourselves invincible" to learn about strategic shift, strategic thinking and strategic adjustment. When there are unfavorable conditions in the competition, we have to wait for the opportunity to defeat the enemy. And when the situation in the market improves, we have to take strategic offensive.

In a word, the enterprise management can benefit a lot from the application of the great wisdom in *The Art of War*.

Case 2

Beijing Tongrentang has staunchly followed the strategic thought of "first make ourselves invincible" to train their staff. In this way, the enterprise has remained prosperous throughout its thirty years of development.

The founder of Tongrentang Le Xianyang used to be a civilian doctor and a vagabond. His philosophy is not to use deception and follow the heart. No matter what he did, he tried to be the best in the same trade, which is the same thought as saying "first make ourselves invincible." All generations of Tongrentang has followed this way of doing things and formed its own unique corporate culture. Le Xianyang believed that the best thing to do was to preserve one's health and do good to society and be a doctor. That is why he named his drugstore *Tongrentang*. His son Le Fengming and his descendents continued his calling and took "preserving people's health and doing good to society" as their duty, treated all honestly and equally. They never cheat on materials and have formed the ethics of doing good to society with great care, which has become the essence of the culture of Tongrentang and been passed down from generation to generation.

The reason why Tongrentang can become the leader in the same industry is that they require that each employee should have their specialties. Take Jia Guichen, the king of ginseng in Tongrentang, for example, relying on his rich experience, he has developed his specialty of distinguishing ginseng. He can tell the quality and origin of any ginseng by a mere look. Many domestic large trade fairs and appraisal meetings always invited him to attend. The ginseng approved by him is often trusted by people who will buy it feeling assured. There are many talents like him in Tongrentang. They are the valued treasure of Tongrentang.

The enterprise spirit of "first make yourself invincible" of Tongrentang includes the following:

First, its quality medicines benefit the patients and satisfy them with its remarkable curative effects

Secondly, its service tenet of "cheating no one neither the old nor the young" has won the trust from the patients.

Thirdly, its unique publicity of promoting porridge in winter and yam in summer has set up a monument for the people.

Case 3

Sun Tzu said: "The skillful warriors in ancient times first made them invincible and then awaited the enemy's moment of vulnerability. Invincibility depends on oneself, but the enemy's vulnerability on himself."

Our Dalian Katelin Specific Alloy Institute is a high-tech enterprise set up in the new situation of reform and opening up. In order to find way out of the predicament and the way to develop at a faster speed to create more wealth to our nation, we have to keep studying, keep up with the strategic plan of the party central committee and according to the party central committee's policy to enrich the people, become rich with hard work and scientific and technological innovation without violating the state's policies and guidelines. In other words, we have to first make ourselves invincible and then plan the development of the enterprise on this basis. It must do good to the nation and people and take the road of common prosperity. Thus, the institute has energetically carried out independent innovation activities, during which time, we have developed three national patents and soon translated the results of scientific researches into productive forces, ridding the institute of trouble and bringing billions of yuan to the nation. In the reform and opening up, our institute has leapt to be a star enterprise known far and wide, mainly benefiting from the strategic thought of "first make yourself invincible" which made us come to see clearly our direction of development—climb the mountain of science under the guidance of the scientific outlook on development by seeking truth from facts. In this way, our institute has increased dozens of times in its output and profit. Our model deeds have been reported by many media. This year is the thirtieth year since the reform and opening up policy was introduced in China and I was luckily awarded "Excellent People in China's Reform."

Change from managing people with systems to self-management that allows people to consciously give play to their potentials, and the enterprise can develop in an invincible position.

-Author's note

Chapter 5
USE OF ENERGY

A good commander attacks the enemy as easily as hitting an egg with a stone. It is because he attacks the enemy's weaknesses with his strengths.

A good commander is able to make use of favorable situations to overwhelm the enemy, the energy of which is as irresistible as the momentum of a round stone rolling down a mountain thousands of feet in height.

Sun Tzu said: Generally, management of a large force is the same in principle as the management of a few men: it is a matter of organization[1]. And to direct a large army to fight is the same to direct a small one: it is a matter of command signs and signals[2]. That the whole army can sustain the enemy's all-out attack without suffering defeat is due to operations of extraordinary and normal forces[3]. Troops thrown against the enemy as a grindstone[4] against eggs is an example of the strong beating the weak.

Generally, in battle, use the normal force to engage[5] and use the extraordinary to win. Now, to a commander adept at the use of extraordinary forces, his resources are as infinite as the heaven and earth, as inexhaustible as the flow of the running rivers. They end and begin again like the motions of the sun and moon. They die away and then are reborn like the changing of the four seasons. There are not more than five musical notes, but the various combinations of the five notes bring about more melodies than can ever be heard[6]. There are not more than five basic pigments[7], yet in blending them together it is possible to produce more colors than can ever be seen. There are not more than five cardinal tastes[8], but the mixture of the five yields more flavors than can ever be tasted. In battle, there are not more than two kinds of postures-operation of the extraordinary force and operation of the normal force, but their combinations give rise to an endless series of maneuvers, for these two forces are mutually reproductive[9]. It is like moving in circle, never coming to an end. Who can exhaust the possibilities of their combinations?

When torrential water[10] tosses boulders, it is because of its momentum; when the strike of a hawk breaks the body of its prey[11], it is because of timing[12]. Thus, in battle, a good commander creates a posture releasing an irresistible and overwhelming momentum, and his attack is precisely timed in a quick tempo. The energy is similar to a fully drawn crossbow[13]; the timing, the release of the trigger[14].

Amid turmoil and tumult of battle, there may be seeming disorder[15] and yet no real disorder in one's own troops. In the midst of confusion and chaos[16], your troops appear to be milling about in circles, yet it is proof against defeat[17].

Apparent disorder is born of order; apparent cowardice, of courage; apparent weakness, of strength[18]. Order or disorder depends on organization and direction[19]; courage or cowardice on postures[20]; strength of weakness on dispositions[21].

Thus, one who is adept at keeping the enemy on the move maintains deceitful appearances[22], according to which the enemy will act. He lures with something that the enemy is certain to take. By so doing he keeps the enemy on the move and then waits for the right moment to make a sudden ambush with picked troops.

Therefore, a skilled commander sets great store by using the situation to the best advantage, and does not make excessive demand on him subordinates. Hence he is able to select right men and exploits the situation[23]. He who takes advantage of the situation uses his men in fighting as rolling logs or rocks. It is the nature of logs and rocks to stay stationary on the flat ground, and to roll forward on a slope. If four-cornered, they stop; if round-shaped, they roll. Thus the energy developed by good fighting men is as the momentum of a round stone rolling down a mountain thousands of feet in height. This is what we call "energy."

5.1 Notes

1. Organization: the organization of army. As long as the organization is rigorous, the direction of army is the same regardless of its size.

2. Command signs and signals: order given by beating a drum or waving the flags. The soldiers act according to the drum and the flag, thus there will come no disorder no matter how many soldiers there are in the army.

3. Extraordinary and normal forces: normal means standard while extraordinary signifies changes

4. Grindstone: whetstone

5. Engage: engage in a war.

6. Five musical notes: the five musical notes in ancient music is gong, shang, jiao, zhi, yu, corresponding roughly to do, re, mi, sol, la.

7. Five basic pigments: they are green, yellow, red, white and black.

8. Five cardinal tastes: they are sour, salty, pungent, bitter and sweet.

9. These two forces are mutually reproductive: the two forces can transform into each other.

10. Torrential water: water that runs with tremendous force.

11. Breaks the body of its prey: destroy the prey.

12. Timing: temperance, proper limits

13. Fully drawn crossbow: a crossbow drawn to its limit ready to be released.

14. The release of the trigger: send.

15. Amid turmoil and tumult of battle: fight amid turmoil.

16. In the midst of confusion and chaos: the battle in is chaos.

17. Your troops appear to be milling about in circles, yet it is proof against defeat: milling about in circles means the troops turned into round formation to defend themselves. The round formation where the head and the tail of the troops meet enables the troops to move freely. It is a formation that is good for defense and not easily defeated.

18. Apparent disorder is born of order; apparent cowardice, of courage; apparent weakness, of strength: if the army wants to pretend to be in chaos to the enemy, it must be itself rigorous; to be coward, be brave itself and to be weak, be strong itself.

19. Order or disorder depends on organization and direction: the

formation and organization of the army decides whether it is in neat formation or in chaos.

20. Courage or cowardice on postures: the army's situations in the battle decide whether the soldiers are brave or coward.

21. Strength of weakness on dispositions: the military strength of the army decides its fighting capacity.

22. Maintains deceitful appearances: make the enemy act by deception.

23. Exploits the situation: make use of all favorable situations.

5 .2 Explanation

Sun Tzu said: the reason why one can manage a large force as freely as manage a small one is that its military formation and organization are reasonable. The reason why one can direct a large force to fight as well as direct a small one is due to its conspicuous flags, resounding drum and smooth communication. The key to not being defeated in an all-out attack is the operation of extraordinary and normal forces. A master of war can attack the enemy as easily as hit an egg with stone. And the reason lies in striking the weak with the strong.

Generally in battle, the normal force is used to engage while the extraordinary force is used to win. The commander good at using the extraordinary force to win changes his tactics as infinitely as the heaven and earth change and as the four seasons alternate. There are merely five musical notes (gong, shang, jiao, zhi, yu), but their various combinations can compose endless music. There are only five basic colors (green, red, yellow, white and black), but the blending of the five colors can produce many colorful beautiful pictures. There are only five cardinal tastes (pungent, sour, salty, bitter and sweet) but the mixture of them can make countless diverse tasty delicacies. Though there are only two tactics: the operations of normal and extraordinary forces, but their combination can generate an infinite number of maneuvers, for they can transform into each other. This change is like moving in circle, never coming to an end. Who can exhaust the possibilities of their combinations?

The torrents can move boulders due to its great momentum. The hawk can kill its prey due to its goo timing. Therefore, a master of war creates a situation that can release an irresistible and overwhelming momentum. And his attack is precisely timed in a quick tempo. Such a situation is just like a fully drawn crossbow whose arrow is going to be shot at a trigger. Directing a battle amid turmoil and tumult requires the commander's army to be in order. While in the midst of confusion and chaos, the army should be in round formation so that they can move freely and be put in an invincible position.

If the army is overly neatly formed, it will lose its agility, which will make itself fail to deal with the changes in battle and in the end be landed in chaos. Being too brave always engenders the fear of failure and being too powerful generates psychological weakness. Neatness and chaos depends on formation and command. Bravery and cowardice is the outer reflection of the quality of the soldiers. And the strength and weakness reflects the military strength.

Hence, a commander adept in keeping the enemy on the move makes use of false appearance, according to which the enemy will act. By holding out baits that the enemy is certain to take, he keeps the enemy on the move and then waits for the right moment to destroy them with a body of picked men.

Therefore, a skilled commander always tries to create favorable situations and does not demand perfection in his subordinates. Hence, he can choose the right men and create and exploits favorable situations. He who can take advantage of the favorable situations operates the war as rolling logs or rocks. It is the nature of logs and rocks to stay stationary on the flat ground, and to roll forward on a slope. If four-cornered, they stop; if round-shaped, they roll. Hence, energy developed by a good commander is irresistible as the momentum of a round stone rolling down a mountain thousands of feet in height.

5.3 Analysis

This chapter's title "Use of Energy" means to make the army form a powerful energy through the art of command and operation. This energy is a strong momentum that overwhelms the enemy.

The core of this chapter is the repeated use of normal and extraordinary forces to defeat the enemy in an unexpected way. By subjective initiative, a commander combines the normal force and the extraordinary force to create a favorable situation in the battle. The three chapters related to "disposition," "energy," and "weaknesses and strengths" cooperate with each other and form the living soul of *The Art of War*.

"Energy" is a dynamic function created by men using the objective conditions. Once formed, it becomes a power that can overwhelm the enemy.

Despite powerful, the energy's formation cannot be finished without the art of correct and flexible operations of normal and extraordinary forces. Thus, people can make use of the power of energy to serve the needs of war.

An excellent strategist can win the war due to his ability of creating and exploiting energy. Creating energy means to make use of the objective conditions to create "energy" that may deter the enemy. While exploiting energy means to translate this "energy" into great power to defeat the enemy and win the war.

So what is the essence of "energy"? Sun Tzu said: "In battle, there are not more than two kinds of postures-operation of the extraordinary force and operation of the normal force, but their combinations give rise to an endless series of maneuvers, for these two forces are mutually reproductive." The energy in war is the inner paradoxical movement of the laws of war. In battle, it is the flexible use of operations and creativity. The operation of the greatest fighting capacity can defeat the enemy due to the fact that it is the integration of creating energy and exploiting energy. Sun Tzu has made a series of analogies to show what the energy is and its power. He said that "when torrential water tosses boulders, it is because of its momentum; when the strike of a hawk breaks the body of its prey, it is because of timing." Therefore, the commander good at making use of energy can tactfully use the limited power to create an irresistible energy and give full play to its great fighting capacity.

Then how does one "create energy" and "exploit energy"? It needs to skillfully use the normal and extraordinary forces. To exploit energy is to observe the objective laws and take advantage of them. By making the best of the situations, a good commander does not make excessive demand on his subordinates. Hence he is able to select right men and exploits the situation. All the strategies in the past battles such as "catch an enemy off guard with a surprise attack," "making a feint to the east and attacking in the west," "sowing discord among the enemy," "deceiving the enemy by torturing one's own man," "presenting a bold front to conceal unpreparedness," "killing someone with a borrowed knife," are good examples of making good use of the operations of normal and extraordinary forces to create deceitful appearances to the enemy and strike the enemy's weaknesses with strengths. Under the situation of knowing the enemy and yourself and striking the enemy's weaknesses with your strengths, to attack the enemy is as easy as to hit an egg with a stone and cut a watermelon with a knife. It is quite an easy thing to win the war.

Flow in language and full of appropriate analogies and argument, this chapter is a beautiful literature masterpiece that can serve as a commander in both war and all industries.

5.4 Cases

Case 1

One thing that directing troops, governing people and managing business have in common is playing to the score. Take directing the army as an example, his enemies and environment are changing all the time. Thus, the commander has to adopt different strategies according to the different enemies. Only by skillfully operating the normal and extraordinary forces can the commander win the victory. Sun Tzu said that generally in battle, use the normal force to engage and use the extraordinary to win. By using the extraordinary force, we can attack the enemy unprepared. The same goes with operating business.

After a dozen of years of fierce competition, our market of washing machines has already been saturated. Many enterprises have closed their doors. As all the washing machines sold in the market are high-capacity and power-consuming ones, and sell well in spring and autumn, if no innovation is made in the market, sales of the products will decline. Seizing the new business opportunity, Haier blazed a trail to develop a small-capacity power-saving washing machine called "prodigy." Once put into market, "prodigy" washing machines are salable, with a million sold within twenty months after it was launched. And after six improvements, the product better serves the different consumer demands of different users.

Swimming in the ocean of business, you have to know the temperature of the water, the strength of the wind and the height of the tide to make the right plan so that you can survive the storm and make unexpected achievements in it. This is just the same with flexibility using normal and extraordinary forces to put oneself in an invincible position in the art of war.

In order to improve its competitiveness, modern enterprises have to promote with great efforts the innovation in system, management, thinking pattern, thoughts, service mode and products. In modern society, we should see both the cruelty of competition and the infinity of opportunity. Not seeing the forest for the trees cannot help us to see the new opportunities. As an excellent entrepreneur, he should be far-sighted, think independently with new ideas, and predict the potential market demands according to the law of the development of market. Only in this way can he seize the opportunity to seek greater development and be surprised to find that the opportunity is close at hand. Without a strategic vision, the thought of flexible operation of normal and extraordinary forces, one will turn a blind eye to the opportunity and miss it even if the opportunity is right in front of him.

In business war, in order to achieve unexpected results by flexibly operating normal and extraordinary forces, one has to do the following:

1. Avoid the enemy's strength and strike his weakness; to seize the market by destroying the rivals one by one. When the Japanese company Canon competed with Xerox for the market in London, Canon adopted the strategy of avoiding the enemy's strength and striking its weakness. When Xerox was tightly controlling the market in London, Canon did not confront Xerox. Instead, it focused its strength to seize the market in Scotland and other areas in Britain. Meanwhile, it has secretly improved the quality of its products which had won themselves relatively high publicity. And finally Canon decided to seize the market in London with its superiority and kicked Xerox out of London in 1980s.

2. In military war and business war, only by using extraordinary force to win can one overwhelm the enemy. It is better to put all the eggs in several baskets than put them all in one basket, for even if you fail in one field you may succeed somewhere else. For instance, when developing its domestic and overseas markets, Haier Group has developed different markets and succeeded in seizing the market.

   The President of Wanxiang Group Lu Guanqiu finished his initial primitive accumulation by producing plowshares, rakes, cardan joints and paraffin steel in the mill-style production mode. In 1979, Lu Guanqiu began to adjust his strategies. He abandoned the mill-style business operation and focused on the specialized production of cardan joints. Thus, the enterprise had entered the growth stage of specialized production and modernized management. In 1980 when in financial strain, the enterprise paid special attention to its quality and the passing rates of the products had reached 99.4%, topping the industry in China. As it has concentrated its own strength to compete in its specialty, the enterprise has received remarkable economic benefits. Between 1980 and 1989, the economic benefits made from cardan joints increased by 40% each year.

In 1989, Lu Guanqiu bought out the stock rights of cardan joints from Ningwei government with RMB15,000,000. In 1990, he set out the strategic policy of "large group strategy, small accounting system, capital operation and international market." He put the "qianchaobei" cardan joints into the markets in eighteen countries and regions such as Japan, Italy, France, Australia and Hong Kong. These products brought him more than $2,290,000 worth of foreign exchange each year. On this basis, Lu Guanqiu expanded from the manufacturing industry to capital market. In 1993, the company was listed and Wanxiang America Corporation was set up in America in 1994.

In 1997, the cardan joints they produced had opened the door of the world's auto giant General Motors and become the first China enterprise that provided products to GM. In recent years, by combing developing industry and capital operation such as trading stock rights for market, equipment for markets and buying intangible assets, the company used the skill of using the normal force to engage and using the extraordinary to win to set up eighteen companies successively in seven countries such as America, Britain, Germany and Canada and gradually blended into the international market. Its revenues in 2007 has exceeded RMB40 billion. At present, the company is marching into the market of high-tech industry and automobile industry.

3. When your rival in a market is superior to yourself, you should lure him to compete in the market that benefits yourself. When your rival is extremely powerful, you should blaze a trail to overtake your rival in a field and thus win the competition. When the market of large-size freezers is almost saturated, Haier Group developed a small-size freezer specific to single men which is both cheap and energy-saving. And it suddenly was salable in the European and American markets, which is a good example of correctly using of extraordinary force to win.

To create a favorable posture of operation, one should be good at operating normal and extraordinary forces. "To a commander adept at the use of extraordinary forces, his resources are as infinite as the heaven and earth, as inexhaustible as the flow of the running rivers." "The energy developed by good fighting men is as the momentum of a round stone rolling down a mountain thousands of feet in height. This is what we call "energy." The impact of the torrents and boulders falling from high mountains are tremendous. In market economy, large enterprises are blockbusters in the market by virtue of their solid strength and leading technology. Afraid to confront them, other enterprises shrink back from difficulties. Thus large enterprises can "subdue the enemy without fighting." This is an example of using energy to win without fighting, which has great impact on the course and result of competition.

However, small enterprises should not be pessimistic. They should set up their superior projects with their core competitiveness and have their own characteristics. Only in this way can they have competitiveness. Large enterprises have their difficulties and small ones have their advantages as well.

Bill Gates' Microsoft Corporation started from a company of three persons and one dollar. And China's Neusoft Group developed from a company of three teachers from Northeastern University, three computers and RMB 30,000. As long as an enterprise has its own characteristics and market potential, it can also defeat the enemy with a force inferior in number or strike the enemy with a weaker force. By proceeding from reality and need with the attitude of being realistic and practical and creating "energy," its opportunity will roll bigger and bigger as a snowball.

Wahaha developed since it had successfully opened its market in South China by launching nutrient solution for children in 1980s. China is a large country with a population of 1.3 billion. It has an enormous market potential. How does it open its markets in Middle China, Northeast China and North China? Wahaha adopted the policy of first creating a posture and then capturing the market. It first gave each pupil in Zhengzhou a yellow hat to remind motor vehicles and bicycles of paying attention to the safety of the students crossing the road. But the hats given away were branded the name of Wahaha, which is a cheap yet good means of publicity for they had won favorable impression from the citizens and the parents of the students. Thus it was not surprising that they would accept its products.

As the whole nation loves the Spring Festive Gala, Wahaha further created its posture by sponsoring the gala. Therefore, its products were soon promoted across China and seized the market in North China and then the whole country with great momentum.

Case 2

Sun Tzu said: generally, in battle, use the normal force to engage and use the extraordinary to win. Now, to a commander adept at the use of extraordinary forces, his resources are as infinite as the heaven and earth, as inexhaustible as the flow of the running rivers.

In battle, there are not more than two kinds of postures-operation of the extraordinary force and operation of the normal force, but their combinations give rise to an endless series of maneuvers.

By following the principle of operating normal and extraordinary forces in *The Art of War*, our institute has made many correct decisions. We have yielded twice the result with half the effort and achieved unexpected success.

For instance, in June, 2010, Shandong Jiaonan power plant needed the boiler anti-wear flame plating technology. The plant had come out with two plans: 1) gave the project to their fellow townsmen whose technology was inferior to ours, and 2) gave it to us for our technology was excellent with great performance. And the result of their discussion was: in the evening of June 19, they informed us that if we could participate in the bid meeting before 9 a.m. on June 20, they would give the project to us. Otherwise, their fellow townsmen would get it. They planned to catch us unprepared, believing that we could not make it there. But we surprised them. There is a sea between Shandong and Liaoning. Usually one cannot arrive in Shandong from Liaoning at 9 a.m. But I booked an air ticket via Internet to fly from Dalian International Airport at 7a.m. the next morning directly to Qingdao. When I arrived in Qingdao Liuting Airport, it was 8:00 in the morning. Without breakfast, I hailed a taxi and reached Jiaonan Power Plant at 8:30. The leader was taken aback when he saw me arrive on time. We didn't expect that you can arrive so soon since we just informed you last night. If you did not make it here today, we are going to give the project to the local people. Since you have made it here and in view of your excellent technology, we feel assured to give the project to you. Due to my unexpected arriving on time, a practice of "use the normal force to engage and use the extraordinary to win," we signed a contract worth RMB500,000. It is exactly "to a commander adept at the use of extraordinary forces, his resources are as infinite as the heaven and earth, as inexhaustible as the flow of the running rivers." We have achieved success by using extraordinary force.

Case 3

Sun Tzu said: "When torrential water tosses boulders, it is because of its momentum; when the strike of a hawk breaks the body of its prey, it is because of timing. Thus, in battle, a good commander creates a posture releasing an irresistible and overwhelming momentum, and his attack is precisely timed in a quick tempo. The energy is similar to a fully drawn crossbow; the timing, the release of the trigger." Sun Tzu praised high of the ability of hawk. Thus, till now, there are hawkish people and hawk-style enterprise management. Dalian Katelin Specific Alloy Institute appreciates a lot the hawk-style enterprise management. A country, a nation, and an enterprise should have a large number of hawkish hardliners to participate in the country's social management or the enterprise management, which is a necessity in today's even tomorrow's development. Hawkish people are ironhanded persons. They are strong in character, decisive and serious. They never compromise on problems related to their principles. And they are as good as their words. Both Chairman Mao and Comrade Deng Xiaoping are typical hawkish supermen. They never compromised on problems related to principles and on issues related to sovereignty. They have never been irresolute when firmness is needed and have shown the steel will of Chinese people. Chairman Mao has led the Chinese to fight against the Japanese and defeated the Japanese imperialism. In the War of Liberation, he led the Chinese to use millet plus rifles to defeat Chiang Kai-shek's eight million well-armed Kuomingtang soldiers. He also led the Chinese to defeat the armed-to-teeth and extremely arrogant U.N. troops in the War to Resist U.S. Aggression and Aid Korea. All of these have shown the hawkish style of Chinese leaders and the undaunted spirit of regarding the imperialism and all reactionaries as paper tiger.

In the reform and opening up, standing high and seeing far, Deng Xiaoping has solved the issue on the returning of the sovereignty of Hong Kong and Macao. With the hawkish style of leadership, he solemnly raised that there is no bargain on the issue of sovereignty. He did not compromise in front of the denial of the imperialists, and finally, the five-star red flag flows high in the sky of Hong Kong and Macao.

A hawkish entrepreneur is not only strict with his employees but also with himself. He will make what others fail to make. He tries to be the model in all respects. Only by respecting himself first can he make the employees respect him.

A hawkish entrepreneur is strict with the employees. The work that can be done today cannot be delayed till tomorrow. The reason why our institute has made so many achievements is that we have hawkish management and strict requirements, especially the strict requirements on managers. Sometimes, in order to finish the task on time, I get up three in the morning and work over 16 hours. Sometimes when I want to have a rest because my eyes were hurt due to long time work, I would force myself to continue to work and not rest till the task is finished. Luckily, all my hard work pays off. Due to my tenacity and taking the lead in striving, this hawkish style of management has fostered a large number of excellent experts and business backbones who are hardworking and not afraid of difficulties. My award as "Dalian Excellent Inventor" in 2009 also derived from my hard work. Anyone who is willing to work hard and strive will be successful in his career. The success is only a matter of time.

It takes not only good thought but also the dedication to science to climb the heights of science.

-Author's note

Chapter 6
WEAKNESSES AND STRENGTHS

The theme of this chapter is to how to avoid the enemy's strength and strike his weakness in war. The commander should take the initiative in war to keep the enemies on move rather than be controlled by them.

The basic guarantee of victory in war is to attack the enemy unprepared and focus your picked forces to attack the enemy forces one by one.

Sun Tzu said: Generally, he who occupies the field of battle first and awaits his enemy is at ease[1]; he who arrives later and joins battle in haste is weary[2]. And, therefore, one skilled in war brings the enemy to the field of battle and is not brought there by him[3].

One able to make the enemy come of his own accord does so by offering him some advantage[4]. And one able to stop him from coming does so by inflicting damage on him[5]. Thus, when the enemy is at ease, he is able to tire him; when well fed, to starve him; when at rest, to make him move[6].

Appear at points which the enemy must hasten to defend[7]; march swiftly to places where you are not expected. That you may march a thousand li (500km) without tiring yourself is because you travel where there is no enemy[8]. That you are certain to take what you attack is because you attack a place the enemy does not or cannot protect. That you are certain of success in holding what you defend is because you defend a place the enemy must hasten to attack.

Therefore, against those skillful in attack, the enemy does not know where to defend, and against the experts in defense, the enemy does not know where to attack.

How subtle and insubstantial, that the expert leaves no trace[9]. How divinely mysterious[10], that he is inaudible. Thus, he is master of his enemy's fate.

His offensive will be irresistible if he plunges into the enemy's weak points[11]; he cannot be overtaken when he withdraws if he moves swiftly[12]. Hence, if we wish to fight, the enemy will be compelled to an engagement even though he is safe behind high ramparts and deep ditches. This is because we attack a position he must relieve[13]. If we do not wish to fight, we can prevent him from engaging us even though the lines of our encampment are merely traced

out on the ground. This is because we divert him from going where he wishes[14].

Accordingly, by exposing the enemy's dispositions and remaining invisible ourselves[15], we can keep our forces concentrated, while the enemy's must be divided. We can form a single united body at one place, while the enemy must scatter his forces at ten places. Thus, it is ten to one when we attack him at one place, which means we are numerically superior. And if we are able to use many to strike few at the selected place, those we deal with will be in dire straits[16]. The spot where we intend to fight must not be made known[17]. In this way, the enemy must take precautions at many places against the attack. The more places he must guard, the fewer his troops we shall have to face at any given point[18]. For if he prepares to the front his rear will be weak; and if to the rear, his front will be fragile. If he strengthens his left, his right will be vulnerable; and if his right gets strengthened, there will be few troops on his left. If he sends reinforcements everywhere, he will be weak everywhere. Numerical weakness comes from having to prepare against possible attacks[19]; numerical strength from compelling the enemy to make these preparations against us[20].

Therefore, if one knows the place and time of the coming battle, his troops can march a thousand li (500km) and fight on the field[21]. But if one knows neither the spot nor the time, then one cannot manage to have the left wing help the right wing or the right wing help the left; the forces in the front will be unable to support the rear, and the rear will be unable to reinforce the front. How much more so if the furthest portions of the troop deployments extend tens of miles in breadth, and even the nearest troops are separated by several miles[22]!

Although I estimate the troops of Yue (an ancient country) as many, of what benefit is this superiority in terms of victory[23]?

Thus, I say that victory can be achieved[24], for even if the enemy is numerically stronger, we can prevent him from fighting.

Therefore, analyze the enemy's battle plan, so as to have a clear understanding of its strong and weak points[25]. Agitate the enemy, so as to ascertain his pattern of movement[26]. Lure him in the open so as to find out his vulnerable spots in disposition[27]. Probe him and learn where his strength is abundant and where deficient[28].

Now, the ultimate in disposing one's troops is to conceal them without ascertainable shape[29]. In this way, the most penetrating spies cannot pry nor can the wise lay plans against you.

Even though we show people the victory gained by using flexible tactics in conformity to the changing situations[30], they do not comprehend this. People all know the tactics by which we achieved victory[31], but they do not know how the tactics were applied in the situation to defeat the enemy[32]. Hence no one victory is gained in the same as another[33]. The tactics change in an infinite variety of ways to suit changes in the circumstances[34].

Now, the laws of military operations are like water[35]. The tendency of water is to flow form heights to lowlands. The law of successful operations is to avoid the enemy's strength and strike his weakness[36]. Water changes its course in accordance with the contours of the land. The soldier works out his victory in accordance with the situation of the enemy[37]. Hence, there are neither fixed postures nor constant tactics in warfare. He who can modify his tactics in accordance with the enemy situation and thereby succeeds in winning may be said to be divine.

Thus, of the five elements (metal, wood, water, fire and earth) none is ever predominant; of the four seasons, none lasts forever; of the days, some are longer and others shorter, and of the moon, it sometimes waxes and sometimes wanes.

6.1 Notes

1. Generally, he who occupies the field of battle first and awaits his enemy is at ease: he who can take up the battle field first and put himself in an active position to wait for the enemy at ease.

2. He who arrives later and joins battle in haste is weary: in battle, he who comes later accept battle in haste and thus becomes weary and is put in the passive position.

3. Brings the enemy to the field of battle and is not brought there by him: maneuver the enemy not the other way round.

4. One able to make the enemy come of his own accord does so by offering him some advantage: the reason why one can make the

enemy come on his own will is because of the bait held out to him.

5. One able to stop him from coming does so by inflicting damage on him: the reason why one can stop the enemies from coming is that he keeps them in check.

6. When at rest, to make him move: if the enemy defends tenaciously, I try to make him move.

7. Appear at points which the enemy must hasten to defend: attack the enemy where they cannot offer reinforcements, i.e. strike his weaknesses.

8. That you may march a thousand li (500km) without tiring yourself is because you travel where there is no enemy: the reason why we can march a thousand li (500km) without feeling tired is that the enemy does not post troops where we go.

9. How subtle and insubstantial, that the expert leaves no trace: if we can make subtle use of the strengths and weaknesses, no trace will be left.

10. How divinely mysterious[10], that he is inaudible: if we can make mysterious use of the strengths and weaknesses, no sound will be left.

11. His offensive will be irresistible if he plunges into the enemy's weak points: the reason that the enemy cannot defend where we attack is that we attack their weaknesses.

12. He cannot be overtaken when he withdraws if he moves swiftly: the reason why we can retreat fast without being overtaken by the enemy is that it is too late for them to chase. Thus the initiative of withdrawing is in our hand.

13. Hence, if we wish to fight … This is because we attack a position he must relieve: if we hope to fight a decisive battle with the enemy, he does not have a choice. The reason for this is that the point we choose to attack is his vulnerable point.

14. This is because we divert him from going where he wishes: keep the enemy on the move in the direction contrary to his wish.

15. Accordingly, by exposing the enemy's dispositions and remaining invisible ourselves: not showing our true dispositions.

16. Those we deal with will be in dire strait: if we can use many to strike few at the selected place, the enemy we are going to attack will be vulnerable.

17. The spot where we intend to fight must not be made known: nobody knows where we are going to fight.

18. In this way, the enemy must take precautions at many places against the attack. The more places he must guard, the fewer his troops we shall have to face at any given point: as the enemy does not know where we are going to attack, he must take precautions at many places against the attack. Therefore, their forces are scattered and the enemy's forces in some parts are weak and thus it is for us to win the victory there.

19. Numerical weakness comes from having to prepare against possible attacks: the reason why the forces are relatively weak is that his forces are scattered to take precautions at different places against possible attacks.

20. Numerical strength from compelling the enemy to make these preparations against us: the reason why the forces are relatively strong is that he forces the enemies to scatter their forces to prepare against possible attacks.

21. Therefore, if one knows the place and time of the coming battle, his troops can march a thousand li (500km) and fight on the field: if we can know the geographical conditions and the time for battle before the battle, we can march a thousand li (500km) to fight with the enemy.

22. But if one knows neither the spot nor the time...even the nearest troops are separated by several miles: if we cannot know the place and the time of the coming battle, we cannot manage all the forces to help each other, not to mention that the operation is often conducted several or even a dozen of miles away.

23. Of what benefit is this superiority in terms of victory: though the number of the soldiers in Yue is large, they do not know how to use of the many and the few, how could it benefit them to win the victory?

24. Victory can be achieved: we can create conditions to win victories.

25. Analyze the enemy's battle plan, so as to have a clear understanding of its strong and weak points: I should carefully calculate the enemy's battle plan to have a good understanding of the strong and weak points of the plan.

26. Agitate the enemy, so as to ascertain his pattern of movement: provoke the enemy to know about his pattern of action.

27. Lure him in the open so as to find out his vulnerable spots in disposition: use deception to lure the enemy in order to find out his strengths and weaknesses.

28. Probe him and learn where his strength is abundant and where deficient: have a tentative rival of strength with the enemy to find out their weaknesses and strengths.

29. Now, the ultimate in disposing one's troops is to conceal them without ascertainable shape: we show the enemy the deceitful disposition of our troops, therefore leaving no trace of our true disposition.

30. Even though we show people the victory gained by using flexible tactics in conformity to the changing situations: we win the victory by using flexible tactics according to the enemy's situations and show the victory to people.

31. People all know the tactics by which we achieved victory: people only know how we overcome the enemy.

32. But they do not know how the tactics were applied in the situation to defeat the enemy: but they do not know the secret how we defeat the enemy.

33. Hence no one victory is gained in the same as another: therefore the tactics we use to defeat the enemy never repeat.

34. The tactics change in an infinite variety of ways to suit changes in the circumstances: circumstances, the enemy's situation.

35. The laws of military operations are like water: the law of using troops is like the law of the movement of water.

36. The law of successful operations is to avoid the enemy's strength and strike his weakness: the principle of using troops is to avoid the enemy's strong points and attack his weak points.

37. Water changes its course in accordance with the contours of the land. The soldier works out his victory in accordance with the situation of the enemy: the flow direction of water is subject to the topography of the land and the way to achieving victory in war depends on the situation of the enemy.

6.2 Explanation

Sun Tzu said that in battle, the one who takes over the battle field first can wait for the enemy at ease and the one who comes later accepts the battle in haste and thus becomes weary. Thus, an excellent commander always tries to keep the enemy on the move rather being brought to the battle field by the enemy.

We need to offer some advantage to make the enemy come to the battle field we have chosen. The reason why we can stop the enemy from arriving at the chosen spot is that we have set many obstacles for him. If the enemy waits at ease for our exhaustion, we should try to tire him. If he is abundant in provisions, we should try to starve him and if he is at rest, we should try to disturb him.

Attack the places where the enemy does not set up defenses. Strike him at the time and in the places the enemy does not expect. The reason why we can march a thousand li (500km) without feeling tired is that the enemy does not set up defenses where we travel. The reason why we are certain to take what we attack is that the place we attack is the place the enemy doesn't take precautions against. And the reason why we can firmly defend ourselves is that the place we defend is the one the enemy is not able to attack.

Thus he who is skilled at attacking can make the enemy feel at a loss as to how to defend. While he who is skilled at defending can make the enemy not know how to attack.

How subtle it is to make the trace of our troops invisible to the enemy! And how mysterious it is to make the sound of our troops inaudible to the enemy! That explains why we can be the master of the enemy.

That the enemy cannot defend where we attack is because the place we attack is the enemy's weak point. That we can retreat without being overtaken by the enemy is that we move swiftly. If we wish to attack the enemy, the enemy has no choice but accept the battle no matter how high the city wall is and how deep the ditches are. This is because the place we attack is the one the enemy must rescue. If we do not wish to fight, we can keep the enemy from engaging us even if we only mark a line to defend. This is because we make the enemy fail to find out where he should attack.

Thus, we can concentrate our forces and divide the enemy's by exposing their disposition and conceal ours. We can focus our forces at one place while the enemies are scattered at ten places. In this way, it is ten to one when we attack him at one place, which means we are numerically superior. And if we can use many to strike few at the place we aim to attack, the forces of the enemy we fight are relatively weak. As the place we plan to attack in unknown to the enemy, the enemy will take precautions against possible attacks in many places. The more places they set up defenses, the more divided their forces are, and the fewer forces we will confront, for if he prepares to the front his rear will be weak; and if to the rear, his front will be fragile. If he strengthens his left, his right will be vulnerable; and if his right gets strengthened, there will be few troops on his left. If he sends reinforcements everywhere, he will be weak everywhere. The reason why the enemy's forces become weak is that he has to passively take precautions against our attack. And the reason why our forces are strong is that we try to make the enemy set up defenses against us everywhere.

Thus, if we know the place and time of the coming battle, we can march a thousand li (500km) and fight on the field. But if otherwise, we cannot have the left wing help the right wing, the right wing help the left, the front help the rear or the rear help the front. How much more so when the nearest distance between the troops is several miles while the farthest one is a dozen of miles!

According to my estimate, though Yue has many troops, what is the benefit it can bring to the victory in the war? Therefore, we can achieve victory by preventing them from joining the fighting and thus deprive them of fighting capacity.

That is why we need to carefully plan to analyze the strong and weak points of the enemy's plan, why we need to agitate the enemy to understand his pattern of movement and why we need to find out the where his forces is strong and where his forces is weak.

So by making the ultimate use of luring the enemy with deception, we can arrive at the best state of not exposing ourselves. In this way, no matter how penetrating the spies are, they cannot find out our plans and lay plans against us to win the victory.

Even if we show the people the victory, they cannot understand the secret of the victory. Everyone knows the process of our defeating the enemy, but they do not know the subtlety of this. Thus, the tactics used to defeat the enemy never repeat. They change in an infinite variety of ways according to the different circumstances of the enemy.

The operation of troops is like the movement of water which flow from heights to lowlands. The law of successful operation is to strike the enemy's weaknesses. Water changes its course in accordance with the contours of the land, while the commander decides the place to attack according to the strengths and weaknesses of the enemy. Hence, there are no fixed postures in warfare, just as water does not have fixed shape or flow direction. It can be said to be divine if we can win the victory by adopting tactics corresponding to the changes of the enemy's situation.

The five elements (metal, wood, water, fire and earth) generate and restrict each other. None is ever predominant. Then four seasons (spring, summer, autumn and winter) alternate. None lasts forever. In the year, the daytime sometimes lasts longer than night while other times shorter. In a day, the moon sometimes waxes and sometimes wanes. Changes are absolute while invariability is relative and temporary.

6.3 Analysis

The theme of this chapter is to discuss how to avoid the enemy's strengths and strike his weaknesses in military, how to master the strengths and the weaknesses, how to transform them how to use the strengths to take the initiative in war and how to bring the enemy to the field of battle and is not brought there by him. Thus, the basic principle of operation of war is raised here --- avoid the enemy's strength and strike his weaknesses.

First of all, we need to try to keep the enemy on the move and not be maneuvered by the enemy. Thus we can wait for the enemy's exhaustion at ease.

The main argument in this chapter is to flexibly use the principle of avoiding the strengths and striking the weaknesses in war so as to win the victory. It is the guarantee of victory to attack the enemy where he does not expect and is not prepare and focus our picked soldiers to defeat them ten to one in all aspects.

The essence of this chapter is that there are no fixed postures in warfare just as water does not have fixed shape. Similarly in business war, one has to flexibly adopt different tactics according to the real conditions to defeat the enemy.

In view of time and space, the chapter attaches great importance of taking the initiative in war. It supports to avoid the enemy's strengths and strike his weaknesses. It emphasizes bringing the enemy to the field of battle and being not brought there by him. One should adopt different tactics to defeat the enemy according to the different situations so that the enemy cannot find out any law about your tactics.

The premise of correct use of strengths and weaknesses is to understand the various expressions of strengths and weaknesses. it needs to give play to one's subjective initiative both in military war and enterprise management. In the competition, we should use and transform the conflicts to create the advantageous situation where our forces are strong while the enemies are weak. And then we strike the enemy's weaknesses with our strengths. "When the enemy is at ease, he is able to tire him; when well fed, to starve him; when at rest, to make him move." "Bring the enemy to the field of battle and not be brought there by him." If the enemy's offensive is irresistible, we should avoid it rather than confront it. When the enemy's provisions are sufficient, burn them so that the enemy will become confused without even going into battle. By tiring and starving the enemy and attacking them at this time, we are certain to win the victory.

The basic principle of using strengths and weaknesses is to change the tactics in an infinite variety of ways according to the enemy situation and thereby succeed. The commander skilled in operating soldiers will formulate strategies according to the changes in the enemy's strengths and weaknesses, avoiding the strengths and striking the weaknesses, and thus achieves the ultimate state of operating the troops as God. "There are neither fixed postures nor constant tactics in warfare. He who can modify his tactics in accordance with the enemy situation and thereby succeeds in winning may be said to be divine." In fact, there is nothing divine. It is merely a combination of the subjectivity and objectivity.

Only by mastering the law of operations can we flexibly apply the law and reach the divine state. In order to freely operate the troops, we have to explore the laws, do things according to the objective laws, give full play to our subjective initiative and play the score. Operating troops as God is to freely apply tactics to deal with the ever changing situations and thus win the victory in war.

"Disposition of Military Strength," "Use of Energy" and this chapter compose the three integral living souls of the art of war.

6.4 Cases

Case 1

Sun Tzu said: "And, therefore, one skilled in war brings the enemy to the field of battle and is not brought there by him."

The value of life is to constantly strive for and create a valuable life. In order to succeed, we have to move forward without being interfered by others. In order to succeed, we have to make use of the wisdom of excellent talents. Therefore, we have to be able to make others on the move rather than be maneuvered by others. All successful men have their own set of abilities to achieve their goals. Our institute is a high-tech enterprise. Therefore, it requires quite a number of talents to cooperate to finish some major research projects. It needs the wisdom and abilities of many talents to constantly make innovations, bloom and bear fruits on the road of science.

Thus, our institute has to hire all kinds of excellent experts with high pay.

For instance, in the research project of energy conservation and emission reduction, our institute has hired experts in chemistry, mechanics, electricity, combustion, and materials and mobilized each expert's creativity, enthusiasm and team spirit to finish the project. The reason why our projects have been valued by the country and listed as national major projects is that our experts are professionally excellent, visionary and have contributed great to the practice of low carbon economy in China.

Our institute has research teams composed of academicians, senior engineers, professors and tutors of doctoral students, with academicians as the academic leaders. The academicians make use of their prestige and personal charisma to organize team members to cooperate with each other to work on the projects and have made rich scientific achievements.

The correct use of the principle of bringing the enemy to the field of battle and not brought there by him" can lead to great success in scientific research.

Case 2

In a big city in China, there are two specialty shops of cheap products. One is called Limin Discount Store whose owner is Ma Tong and the other is called Liguo Discount Store whose owner is Wang Ke. The two stores are next to each other and the two owners have been selling cheap products here from their youths. But they have been treating each other as enemy. For a long time, the fierce competition between the two stores has attracted a lot of consumers to buy cheap products.

One day, Liguo Discount Store put up an advertisement in its showcase that read: cheap linen sheets for sale: RMB13/sheet. Seeing this, the citizens there spread the news around the city and all went to buy the sheets. As usual, soon its next store Limin Discount Store conspicuously put up another advertisement in its showcase that read: our sheets are better and cheaper, only RMB 12/sheet.

Once the advertisement was seen, people all swarmed to Limin Discount Store and bought all the products there.

Competition like this never ends between the two stores. Sometimes Ma Tong prevailed and sometimes Wang Ke took the upper hand. And local residents also expected their competition, for it would bring them good luck so that they could buy very cheap products. Besides putting up advertisement to force prices down, the owners of the two stores often called each other's names outside their own store, sometimes even fought each other, which was really fierce. Finally, this fierce "competition" between the two came to an end when one of them was defeated. When the fight was over, the customers went to the store whose products sold cheaper and bought all of the cheap products. The customers felt comfortable with whatever products they bought and the number of customers increased.

The conflict between the two stores never ceased. Their constant fights had brought huge benefits to the local residents who had bought various cheap and good products. People always hoped that the owners of the two stores would fight again so that they could benefit from it. It has become an indispensible episode in the life of the nearby residents.

Now decades have passed and the owners of the two stores have entered their old years. All of a sudden, one day, the owner of Limin Discount Store disappeared and the store was locked up.

Before long, the owner of Liguo Discount Store put up his store for auction and moved somewhere else. Since then, the nearby residents have never seen the two eccentrics that had brought them excitement and benefits.

One day, when a new owner came to clear up the store, one thing unexpected was found. There was a secret passage between the two stores and a door connects the bedrooms of the two owners. People were surprised and wondered why the bedrooms of the former rivals would be connected.

After an investigation, the finding was to everybody's surprise. The two "mortal enemies" were brothers. Their verbal abuse and fights were put on to attract more customers. All the fights were fraud. No matter which of the two won, the other could sell out all his products. The two stores were actually one. For the past decades, they had made use of the customers' psychology of looking for the cheap and finally won the customers' purchasing psychology by putting constant "fights." Their busy business had brought them a huge amount of money and now they have bought a luxury villa where the two brothers will enjoy their rest of life.

The secret of their success lies in the use of the principles of "nothing is too deceitful in war" and "avoid the enemy's strengths and strike his weaknesses."

They concealed the truth and deceived the customers with the false fight which made the customers feel delighted to buy their cheap products.

Case 3

Sun Tzu said: "Now, the laws of military operations are like water. The tendency of water is to flow form heights to lowlands. The law of successful operations is to avoid the enemy's strength and strike his weakness. Water changes its course in accordance with the contours of the land. The soldier works out his victory in accordance with the situation of the enemy. Hence, there are neither fixed postures nor constant tactics in warfare. He who can modify his tactics in accordance with the enemy situation and thereby succeeds in winning may be said to be divine."

When Dalian Katelin Specific Alloy Institute was first set up, it had a weak economic foundation and was in dire need of funds. How could we get out of the trouble soon? We could sit doing nothing hoping for miracle. We had to rely on ourselves. Under such circumstances, we adopted the approach of avoiding the enemy's strengths and striking his weaknesses." We temporarily avoided large enterprises with great technical strength and targeted our technical service at relatively weak SMEs and township enterprises, which has received unexpected effects. At that time, the brickyards and cement plants that had spread all over were in dire need of our wear resistance technology and thus were very glad to be served by us. There was great scope for the wear-resistant gold dust and welding rod and the wear-resistant alloy spraying process we had developed in township enterprises such as brickyards and cement plants. Soon our technologies were spread all over the township enterprises and for a time, the supply of wear resistance products fell short of the demand. Everyday people from township enterprises came to buy our wear resistance materials and invited our technicians to serve. It had brought abundant start-up capital and got us out of trouble and brought new opportunities to the great development of our institute. The development of the institute owes a lot to the strategic policy of "avoid the strengths and strike the weaknesses." It also inspired us on research projects. Under the guidance of this thought, we have improved the crusher in cement plants and glassworks. The old-fashioned crushers all crush with a single hammer head which strikes only the hard but the soft, a great waste of mechanical energy and poor effect of crushing. Based on these defects, we have changed the single hammer head into multiplex vibration double-crushing wear-resisting alloy hammer head which can crush the hard with one hit and the soft with another hit, with an ideal crushing effect. It has doubled the work efficiency and its quality of crushing is extremely high. Hence, we have applied for technical patent and its patent number is ZL96225033.

Chapter 7
MANEUVERING

This chapter discusses how to strive for favorable conditions and the initiative in war and raises the strategic principle of "make the devious route the most direct and turn disadvantage to advantage," for you will be attacked without taking initiative. Thus, the essence of The Art of War is to contend for the initiative in war.

Sun Tzu said: Normally, in war, the general receives his commands from the sovereign. During the process from assembling the troops and mobilizing the people to deploying the army ready for battle[1], nothing is more difficult that the art of maneuvering for seizing favorable positions beforehand[2]. What is difficult about it is to make the devious route the most direct and to turn disadvantage to advantage[3]. Thus, forcing the enemy to deviate and slow down his march by luring him with bait[4], you may set out after he does and arrive at the battlefield before him. One able to do this shows the knowledge of artifice of deviation.

Thus, both advantage and danger are inherent in maneuvering for an advantageous position[5]. One who sets the entire army in motion with impedimenta to pursue an advantageous position will be too slow to attain it[6]. If he abandons the camp and all the impedimenta to contend for advantage, the baggage and stores will be lost[7].

It follows that when the army rolls up the armor and sets out speedily[8], stopping neither day nor night[9] and marching at double speed[10] for a hundred li (50km) to wrest an advantage, the commander of three divisions will be captured[11]. The vigorous troops will arrive first and the feeble will straggle along behind, so that if this method is used only one-tenth of the army will arrive[12]. In a forced march of fifty li (25km) the commander of the first and van division will fall[13], and using this method but half of the army will arrive[14]. In a forced march of thirty li, but two-thirds will arrive[15]. Hence, the army will be lost without baggage train; and it cannot survive without provisions, nor can it last long without sources of supplies[16].

One who is not acquainted with the design of his neighbors should not enter into alliances with them[17]. Those who do not know the conditions of mountains and forests, hazardous defiles, marshes and swamps, cannot conduct the march of an army. Those who do not use local guides are unable to obtain the advantages of the ground.

Now, war is based on deception[18]. Move, when it is advantageous, and change tactics by dispersal and concentration of your troops[19].

When campaigning, be swift as the wind; in leisurely march, majestic as the forest; in raiding and plundering, be fierce as fire[20]; in standing, be firm as the mountains. When hiding, be as unfathomable as things behind the clouds[21]; when moving, fall like a thunderclap. When you plunder the countryside, divide your forces[22]. When you conquer territory, defend strategic points[23]. Weigh the situation before you move[24]. He who knows the artifice of deviation will be victorious. Such is the art of maneuvering.

The Book of Army Management says: 'As the voice cannot be heard in battle, gongs and drums are used[25]. As troops cannot see each other clearly in battle, flags and banners are used[26]. Gongs and drums, banners and flags, are means whereby the ears and eyes of the host may be focused on one particular point[27]. When the troops can be thus united[28], the brave cannot advance alone, nor can the cowardly retreat. This is the art of handling large masses of men[29]. Hence, in night fighting, usually use drums and gongs; in day fighting, banners and flags, as a means of suiting the soldiers' hearing and sight [30].

A whole army may be robbed of its spirit[31], and its commander deprived of his presence of mind[32]. Now, at the beginning of a campaign, the spirit of soldiers is keen; after a certain period of time, it declines; and in the later stage, it may be dwindled to naught. A clever commander, therefore, avoids the enemy when his spirit is keen and attacks him when it is lost. This is the art of attaching importance to moods[33]. In good order, he awaits a disorderly enemy[34]; in serenity, a clamorous one[35]. This is the art of retaining self-possession. Close to the field of battle, he awaits an enemy coming from afar; at rest, he awaits an exhausted enemy; with well-fed troops, he awaits hungry ones. This is the art of husbanding one's strength[36]. He refrains from intercepting an enemy whose banners are in perfect order[37], and desists from attacking an army whose formations are in an impressive array[38]. This is the art of assessing circumstances[39].

Now, the art of employing troops is that when the enemy occupies high ground, do not confront him uphill[40], and when his back is resting on hills, do not make a frontal attack[41]. When he pretends to flee, do not pursue[42]. Do not attack soldiers whose temper is keen[43]. Do not swallow the bait offered by the enemy[44]. Do not thwart an enemy who is returning homewards[45]. When you surround an army, leave an outlet free[46]. Do not press a desperate enemy too hard. Such is the method of using troops.

7.1 Notes

1. Deploying the army ready for battle: the two armies pitch their camps facing each other.

2. Nothing is more difficult that the art of maneuvering for seizing favorable positions beforehand: the two armies striving for favorable positions.

3. To make the devious route the most direct and to turn disadvantage to advantage: turn the devious route into a straight one and turn the unfavorable conditions into favorable ones.

4. Thus, forcing the enemy to deviate and slow down his march by luring him with bait: in battle, besides making the devious route the most direct and turning disadvantage to advantage, one should also try to make the enemy turn the straight route into a devious one and turn the favorable conditions into unfavorable ones. In order to make this, he has to offer the enemy with bait and thus force him to deviate and be landed in predicament.

5. Both advantage and danger are inherent in maneuvering for an advantageous position: there are good and bad sides about maneuvering.

6. One who sets the entire army in motion with impedimenta to pursue an advantageous position will be too slow to attain it: one cannot attain a favorable position if he leads the entire army to strive for it.

7. If he abandons the camp and all the impedimenta to contend for advantage, the baggage and stores will be lost: the impedimenta will suffer loss if he discards part of the equipment to attain the favorable position.

8. Rolls up the armor and sets out speedily: puts away the armors and marches at full speed.

9. Stopping neither day nor night: march on without rest the whole day

10. Marching at double speed: double their journey without a rest day or night.

11. The commander of three divisions will be captured: if the commander of three divisions orders the army to march for a hundred li (50km) only to strive an advantage, he will be captured by the enemy.

12. The vigorous troops will arrive first and the feeble will straggle along behind, so that if this method is used only one-tenth of the army will arrive: the strong soldiers will arrive first and the feeble ones will lag behind, therefore only one tenth of the entire army will arrive.

13. In a forced march of fifty li (25km) the commander of the first and van division will fall: the commander of the first and van division will be thwarted if he marches fifty li (25km) to contend for the advantageous position.

14. Using this method but half of the army will arrive: in this way, only half of the army can make their way there.

15. In a forced march of thirty li, but two-thirds will arrive: if march thirty li (15km) for the advantageous position, only two thirds of the soldiers can arrive.

16. Nor can it last long without sources of supplies: if the army does not have sufficient supplies, it cannot survive.

17. One who is not acquainted with the design of his neighbors should not enter into alliances with them: if one does not know the plan and intention of his neighboring countries, he should not ally himself with them.

18. War is based on deception: in war, deception should be used to win the victory.

19. Change tactics by dispersal and concentration of your troops: when operating troops in war, one should flexibly disperse or concentrate the troops.

20. In raiding and plundering, be fierce as fire: when attacking the enemy, it is as resistible as the fire blazing the prairie.

21. Be as unfathomable as things behind the clouds: it cannot tell whether it is morning or night when the sun is covered by the clouds.

22. When you plunder the countryside, divide your forces: if you loot food from the enemy's countryside, you have to divide your forces

23. When you conquer territory, defend strategic points: you should open up the field, expand the battle field and divide your troops to take up the favorable position.

24. Weigh the situation before you move: do not take action until you have weighed up the pros and cons.

25. As the voice cannot be heard in battle, gongs and drums are used: gongs ad drums were used to give orders in ancient times. Striking drums means to advance and striking gongs means to withdraw.

26. As troops cannot see each other clearly in battle, flags and banners are used: mainly flags were used in ancient times.

27. Means whereby the ears and eyes of the host may be focused on one particular point: gongs and drums are used to unite the hearing and seeing of the whole army and their action.

28. When the troops can be thus united: when the troops can follow the orders in unity.

29. This is the art of handling large masses of men: this is the way to direct a large number of soldiers.

30. In night fighting, usually use drums and gongs; in day fighting, banners and flags, as a means of suiting the soldiers' hearing and sight: the commanding signal varies from day to night to meet the needs of the hearing and sight of the soldiers.

31. A whole army may be robbed of its spirit: the courage and morale of the entire army can be thwarted and exhausted.

32. Its commander deprived of his presence of mind: the commander's will and determination can be shaken.

33. This is the art of attaching importance to moods: this is the general law of mastering the use of changes in morale.

34. In good order, he awaits a disorderly enemy: keep your own troops in good order to deal with the enemy that is in chaos.

35. In serenity, a clamorous one: use the calm of your troops to deal with the turmoil of the enemy.

36. This is the art of husbanding one's strength: this is the basic way of mastering the use of the solder's fighting capacity.

37. He refrains from intercepting an enemy whose banners are in perfect order: do not attack the enemy whose banners are in good order and whose deployment is thorough.

38. Desists from attacking an army whose formations are in an impressive array: do not attack the enemy whose formation is in an impressive array and whose strength is strong.

39. His is the art of assessing circumstances: this the usual way of dealing with emergencies according to changes.

40. When the enemy occupies high ground, do not confront him uphill: if the enemy has taken up the high ground, do not attack.

41. And when his back is resting on hills, do not make a frontal attack: do not attack the enemy front the front if hills are at his back.

42. When he pretends to flee, do not pursue: do not chase the enemy if he pretends to flee.

43. Do not attack soldiers whose temper is keen: do not attack the enemy's picked army.

44. Do not swallow the bait offered by the enemy: do not attack when the enemy offers small advantage the lure us.

45. Do not thwart an enemy who is returning homewards: do not check

the enemy from the front who is retreating towards their camp.

46. When you surround an army, leave an outlet free: one should leave a gap when besieging the enemy so that the enemy will not fight desperately.

7.2 Explanation

Sun Tzu said that normally in war, the general first receives orders from the ruler and then organizes the troops to confront the enemy on the battlefield. In this process, the most difficult is to attain the opportunity for combat and contend for the favorable conditions. Its difficulty lies in that the general has to turn the devious route into straight one and to turn disadvantageous factors into advantageous ones. Therefore, we have to turn the enemy's route from straight to devious by offering small advantage to lure him to change his line of travel. In this way, we can assure that we can arrive at the battlefield earlier and occupy the favorable position even if we start later than the enemy. One who can make this is the true commander of wisdom who masters the strategy of turning the devious route into straight one.

In contending for advantageous conditions, there are both the possibility of attaining the advantages and the possibility of being landed in dangerous situation. If we set the entire army out with all equipment and impedimenta to contend for the advantage, it is more often than not that we cannot arrive at the planned place on time. But if we abandon the impedimenta to attain the advantage, the equipment will suffer a loss.

Thus, if we roll up the armors to march a hundred li (50km) at full speed to contend for the advantage without a rest day and night, the commander of the three divisions may be captured by the enemy and only one tenth of the soldiers can arrive the destination for the strong ones will arrive first while the feeble ones lag behind. If we march in this way for fifty li (25km) to wrest the advantage, the general of the first and van division will be thwarted and only half of the soldiers will arrive on time. Similarly, if we march thirty li (15km) this way to get the advantage, only two thirds of the army will reach the destination on time. We must know that the army will be destroyed without equipment and impedimenta, that it cannot survive without provisions and that it is certain to be defeated without military supplies.

Without the knowledge of the strategic intent of the neighboring countries, one should not ally himself with them. Without the knowledge of the conditions of mountains, forests, hazardous defiles, marshes and swamps, one cannot conduct the army in war. One cannot attain the favorable geographical location if he does not use the local people as guide. Therefore, in war, we should use deception to win the victory, weighing up the pros and cons before taking action and change tactics by dispersing or concentrating the troops.

In this way, the army can move both as swift as the wind when taking action, and as in good order as forests when marching leisurely. It can be as fierce as fire when attacking, as firm as mountains when defending and as unfathomable as the sun behind the clouds when hiding. And it can move as fast as the thunderclap when moving. When plundering the enemy's countryside, we have to divide the troops and when opening up the territory, we have to divide the forces to defend strategic points and weigh up the advantages and disadvantages before taking action. Only the commander who knows the artifice of deviation will be victorious. Such is the basic principle of contending for advantage.

The Book of Army Management (an ancient book on the art of war) says that as the voice cannot be heard in battle, gongs and drums are used. As troops cannot see each other clearly in battle, flags and banners are used. Thus, gongs and drums are used in night fighting while banners and flags are used in daytime fighting. Gongs, drums, flags and banners are used to unify the action and the strength of the whole army so that neither the brave can advance alone nor the cowardly can retreat. This is the way to operate large masses of soldiers in war.

To the enemy, its morale can be declined and its commander's will and determination can be shaken. Generally, at the beginning of a battle, the spirit of soldiers is keen; after a certain period of time, it declines; and in the later stage, it may be dwindled to naught. A commander skilled at operating troops, therefore, avoids the enemy when his spirit is keen and attacks him when it is lost. This is the way to operate the army according to the moods of the enemy's army. Use the good order of our army to deal with the chaos of the enemy and use our calm to deal with the irascibility of the enemy. This is the way to direct the army according to our psychology and that of the enemy. Make use of our advantage of being close to the field of battle to wait for the enemy coming from afar, make use of our comfort and ease to await an exhausted enemy and take our advantage of being well-fed to wait for the hungry enemy. This is the art of operating the troops by mastering the army's fighting capacity. Do not attack the enemy whose deployment is careful and thorough and whose banners are in perfect order and do not

100

attack the enemy whose formations are in an impressive array. This is the art of operating the troops by meeting the emergencies according to the changes in circumstances.

Hence, the basic principle of operating troops is that when the enemy has occupied the high ground, do not attack him uphill. When his back is resting on hill, do not attack him from the front. When he pretends to flee, do not chase him. Do not rashly attack his picked army or be lured by his bait. When he is retreating homewards, do not check them halfway and leave a gap when besieging him for if you push him too hard he might fight desperately. These are the basic principles of commanding operations.

7.3 Analysis

Maneuvering discusses how to strive for favorable conditions and the initiative in war, raises the strategic principle of "make the devious route the most direct and turn disadvantage to advantage," and puts forward its conditions and requirements. Maneuvering here means to contend for initiative, for you will be attacked without taking initiative. There are skills in maneuvering. To contend for the initiative cleverly and secretly is the essence of *The Art of War*.

Both advantage and danger are inherent in turning the devious route into straight one: "One who sets the entire army in motion with impedimenta to pursue an advantageous position will be too slow to attain it. If he abandons the camp and all the impedimenta to contend for advantage, the baggage and stores will be lost." One cannot abandon the impedimenta for the sake of convenience, otherwise he will be defeated.

"One who is not acquainted with the design of his neighbors should not enter into alliances with them. Those who do not know the conditions of mountains and forests, hazardous defiles, marshes and swamps, cannot conduct the march of an army. Those who do not use local guides are unable to obtain the advantages of the ground." The eight principles of directing troops are: when the enemy occupies high ground, do not confront him uphill, and when his back is resting on hills, do not make a frontal attack. When he pretends to flee, do not pursue. Do not attack soldiers whose temper is keen. Do not swallow the bait offered by the enemy. Do not thwart an enemy who is returning homewards. When you surround an army, leave an outlet free. Do not press a desperate enemy too hard.

This chapter also tells us about the way to "operate troops according to the enemy's psychology, mood and strength." It shows us that man is the main body in a war and his mood, psychology and morale is the key to victory. "Avoid the enemy when his spirit is keen and attack him when it is lost" is a famous saying for myriad years in the art of war and is still of value to commanders today.

Either in military war or business war, the artifice of deviation is the eternal principle of defeating the enemy and winning the victory.

The essence of "maneuvering" is that "two armies contend for advantages," i.e. two armies compete for the conditions of winning the victory and strive for the initiative in the battle. Contending is necessary yet we cannot contend without methods. Otherwise, not only one cannot win but also invite rout to the entire army. Principles such as "to make the devious route the most direct and to turn disadvantage to advantage," "war is based on deception, move, when it is advantageous, and change tactics by dispersal and concentration of your troops," and "avoid the enemy when his spirit is keen and attack him when it is lost" are all thought of dialectics, which require military commanders and excellent entrepreneurs to flexibly use them.

Sun Tzu also presents the patterns of military action. "When campaigning, be swift as the wind; in leisurely march, majestic as the forest; in raiding and plundering, be fierce as fire; in standing, be firm as the mountains. When hiding, be as unfathomable as things behind the clouds; when moving, fall like a thunderclap." He requires us to defeat the enemy with unpredictable skills.

He also proposes the Eight Don'ts: do not confront the enemy uphill when he occupies high ground; do not make a frontal attack when his back is resting on hills; do not pursue when he pretends to flee; do not attack soldiers whose temper is keen; do not swallow the bait offered by the enemy; do not thwart an enemy who is returning homewards; do not leave no outlet free when you surround an army; do not press a desperate enemy too hard.

These excellent military thought are the essence of *The Art of War*.

7.4 Cases

Case 1

The president of Wanxiang Groups Lu Guanqiu was reputed as the entrepreneur going global from farmland. He started from the owner of a blacksmith's shop of three thatched cottages to today's president of a company which produces10.78 million US dollars' worth of foreign exchange. His company's way to success shows the wisdom of an excellent entrepreneur and displays the strong power of applying the principle of "avoid the enemy when his spirit is keen and attack him when it is lost" in *The Art of War* by entrepreneurs in the business war to save an enterprise.

Hangzhou Cardan Joint Plant used to be a blacksmith's shop of only seven workers. It is a small workshop producing sickles, hoes, bearings, rakes and cardan joints. Under the guidance of Lu Guanqiu, though developed to some extent, it still remained an obscure company in China's auto parts industry. The fierce competition exhausted Lu Guanqiu.

In 1979 when the energy was short and auto production declined, the plummet in the sale of auto parts drove Lu Guanqiu's business from bad to worse. The superior authorities advised him to produce bikes. But Lu Guanqiu knew that the competition in bikes was even fiercer. A company like his which is weak in economic foundation could not compete with large companies at all.

Lu knew clearly that a company could only survive in the competition with its own featured products. Since they did not have any then, they had to strive to break new ground.

In the latter part of the 20th century, the energy tension was relieved somewhat due to the development of oil and minerals. Thus the motor transport had developed a lot, which helped the automotive service and auto parts industry developed correspondingly. Hence, the market situation of the production of cardan joints improved.

Lu recognized the gap in the production of cardan joints for imported cars. The gap existed due to the fact that the imported cars' size was complicated, small in production, hard in technology, and few in profit. All the cardan joints of imported cars were imported by the country with foreign exchange. So why not produce cardan joints for imported cars if its production could both avoid the strengths of large companies and meet the emergent demands of the country? This is the correct use of the strategy of "avoid the enemy when his spirit is keen and attack him when it is lost" in *The Art of War*.

Thus, Lu easily got the contract from Beijing China Automotive Company to produce cardan joints for imported cars. After deciding the direction of the company, the whole plant made concerted effort to improve the technology according to high standards and focused all its strength on the production of high-quality cardan joints for imported cars.

After half a year of technological improvement, their first cardan joints were sold out at the National Fair for the Parts of Imported Cars. After years of development, it had become one the three most influential cadan joint manufacturers.

It is really not easy for Wanxiang Group to grow to be a company of today's size by successfully applying the tactics of "avoid the enemy when his spirit is keen and attack him when it is lost."

Case 2

Kroc used to be a poor man who worked for others for a living before finishing junior high school. Later, he worked as a salesman in a factory where he earned more than before. He travelled to many places due to his job as a salesman and had made friends with a lot of people, gained much in knowledge and accumulated much experience in business management, and thus came to have the idea of starting business himself.

The first step is always the hardest. Moreover, Kroc did not have a feasible analysis of which industry to join in. It was only his wish to be self-employed. When trying to figure out which industry to step in, he found himself hungry and wanted to have a meal but no fast-food restaurant could be found. Suddenly, Kroc connected his starting business with fast-food restaurant, thinking that if he could open a fast-food restaurant, the business is sure to be blooming. As the tempo of people's life quickened, the fast food industry would be a hot demand of people.

Now the idea was formed, but the realistic problem he faced was the shortage of money. In real life, every thought is merely a dream if there is not enough money. How difficult it was to open a fast-food restaurant for Kroc who was as poor as a church mouse.

By considering it over and over again, Kroc finally came up with a wonderful idea: as there was no straight road, why not take a devious one? He remembered that he knew the McDonald brothers who were owners of a restaurant when he was a salesman. If he could learn in their restaurant first, it would certainly help to open a restaurant, which was a step closer to his ambition to be a boss.

Once making up his mind, he went to McDonald's. After complimenting the McDonald brothers' restaurant over tea in a private room in the restaurant, Kroc changed his topic and started to tell them his trouble. Winning their sympathy, he lost no time to plead with the McDonald brothers to allow him to work in the restaurant, saying that he would take whatever job in the restaurant even if as a dish washer, otherwise, his daily life would be in crisis.

During the conversation, Kroc knew what the brothers were thinking. In order to realize his ambition as early as possible, he proposed to work as a salesman besides as an assistant and promised that he would gave 5% of his income as a salesman to the owners. Seeing the profits and as they did need a handyman, the McDonald brothers readily accepted Kroc's request.

As soon as Kroc started to work in the restaurant, he became familiar with business management. In order to get the trust from his bosses, he worked exceptionally hard, working from early in the morning till late at night and willing to do whatever job without a complaint. A soldier that does not aim to be a general is not a good soldier and an employee that does not to aim to be a boss is not a good employee. Kroc considered the McDonald brothers' restaurant as his own restaurant and suggested many times to the brothers to improve the business environment to attract more customers.

Besides, he advised to the brothers to provide special box lunch to deliver to the customers. And he offered to deliver the box lunch and be responsible for the business of selling boxed lunches. In the process of delivering box lunches, he met many powerful figures in the society, including the director of the credit department in the bank.

In order to increase operation revenues, he advised the bosses to install acoustic equipment in the dining hall so that the customers can enjoy light music when dining. He also made great efforts to improve the sanitary condition of food, pay special attention to the quality of the meal and protect the credit of the service. He carefully chose the waiters in the dining hall and employed young and beautiful people to serve the customers in the hall and the homely ones to work in the kitchen. Each of the reform made by Kroc was satisfied by his bosses and from what he did, people formed the good impression that he was honest, trustworthy, hardworking and willing to dedicate. As he was good at management and the business got better and better, the bosses always followed his advice. In the eyes of his bosses, Kroc had become a person that the restaurant could not be without.

Unwittingly, Kroc had worked in the McDonald brothers' restaurant for six years. During the period, he became stronger and stronger and the time for him to realize his ambition was mature. Kroc came to the director of the credit department of the bank to consult how to get loans. The director told him that it needed to collateralize his real estate or an official contract of.

Believing the time was right, Kroc came to the McDonald brothers and proposed his idea that he was willing to buy out all the shares of the restaurant for a high price. After several negotiations, Kroc was finally willing to buy out all the shares of the McDonald brothers' restaurant with 2.7 million US dollars to manage the restaurant himself. Always seeking immediate interests, the McDonald brothers thought: 2.7 million US dollars. What an attractive price. How silly it would be if we do not sign the contract!

Reaching an agreement on the price, the brothers and Kroc signed the contract. Getting the contract, Kroc went to the bank to finish the proceedings of loans. When he got the loans, he used part of them as liquid capital and 2.7 million dollars to pay the McDonald's brothers. From then on, Kroc has become the owner of the restaurant and finally realized his ambition to be a boss.

The second day, the event that the employers were fired by the employee became big news in the local place and Kroc made use of the news to publicize the event; and in the end had increased the publicity of the restaurant. By "making the devious route the most direct and turning disadvantage to advantage," Kroc successfully turned into a millionaire and owner of a restaurant from a pauper, which is really thought-provoking.

After becoming the owner of the restaurant, Kroc did better in operations and management. And in a very short time, he was well-known in America for his new idea of operation and paid off all the loans. After another twenty years of hard-working operation, his restaurant had a total asset of 4.2 billion US dollars and becomes an international restaurant. The operation idea of "making the devious route the most direct and turning disadvantage into advantage" has helped Kroc to realize his value of life.

Case 3

Sun Tzu said: "Those who do not know the conditions of mountains and forests, hazardous defiles, marshes and swamps, cannot conduct the march of an army. Those who do not use local guides are unable to obtain the advantages of the ground."

Whenever we arrive at a new power plant, we will ask the technical leaders of the boiler shop and persons who know about the truth of boilers to take us to the abrasion. And after careful consulting, we will pay special attention to find out the spot that is worn the most seriously and mark it so that we can increase our effort there when flame plating. We will carefully examine each tube for missing one spot means there might be another possibility of tube explosion. Countless experiences and lessons have proved that detail is the key to success. As we are careful in our work, adopt advanced ladder-shaped flame plating, and know very well the problems the boilers used to have, the boilers we flame plated usually can work from two to three years without being overhauled. While the boilers plated by many other units can only last for a year at most. Most of time, the boilers will be broken due to abrasion in four or five months and if used any longer, tube explosion will occur.

Finally, all our hard work pays off. The boilers in power plants we flame plated never experience tube explosion within the guarantee period. Just as the power plants said, the quality of our institute's work is guaranteed and people can use at ease. The expenditure on maintenance can be saved, which has greatly increased the economic benefits.

That detail is the key to success originates from the strategic thought in *The Art of War*. It leads us to new success in our work step by step. This is just what is said in *The Art of War* that those who do not use local guides are unable to obtain the advantages of the ground and that those who do not know the conditions of mountains and forests, hazardous defiles, marshes and swamps, cannot conduct the march of an army.

Case 4

Sun Tzu said: "What is difficult about it is to make the devious route the most direct and to turn disadvantage to advantage. Thus, forcing the enemy to deviate and slow down his march by luring him with bait, you may set out after he does and arrive at the battlefield before him. One able to do this shows the knowledge of artifice of deviation."

Just as what Marx said: "There is no royal road to science, and only those who do not dread the fatiguing climb of its steep paths have a chance of gaining its luminous summits." This is a true portrayal of the strategy of "make the devious route the most direct."

All the scientific achievements our institute has made are gained after having undergone numerous difficulties and dangers. In order to test and verify a scientific data, I, a seventy year old man, climbed up the 37-meter-long rope ladder to go inside the boiler of the power plant. If I fell off, I would have had my body smashed to pieces. But I persevered to climb the ladder step by step despite the danger of death, knowing that there will be no light of victory without climbing the ladder with difficulty. In the end, I came to the top of the boiler and commanded the staff to finish the research project, getting "the scripture of technology."

Another time, I was directing my student to conduct a laser experiment in the laboratory. He over hasted to switch on the power before I put on the protective clothing. In a flash, my eyes were hurt. As we were in the suburb which was far away from the hospital and it was night, we could not see a doctor. My eyes were so hurt that I could not help rolling about on the floor. Seeing this, the student cried. I comforted him saying that any achievement is made at a price. One even has to be ready to dedicate himself to science. Without this spirit, no excellent achievement can be made.

The second day, the student sent me to the hospital. However my eyes still hurt hard and for twenty day in a row, I could not open my eyes. In pain I asked myself: am I going to lose my sight? Is my dear research career going to stop? No! I have to cooperate with the doctor to heal my eyes and live healthily to finish my unfinished research career. Finally, I defeated the serious illness. After recuperation, I dedicated to work again in spite of the dissuasion of my relatives and friends. In the end, I finished my dear research task and won a new research patent numbered: ZL94222154.0, making a contribution to the development of productive forces. Paul is my example and his saying will always inspire me: "feel no torturing regrets for wasted years..." I want to be, under the guidance of the scientific outlook on development, to be a worthy teacher and be the example of the students forever.

The strategy of "make the devious route the most direct" makes me understand that there would be no victory in Chinese revolutionary without the red troops' long march of 25,000 li (12,500km) and that Tang Seng's team would never be able to attain the true scriptures without experiencing eighty one obstacles. In a word, all achievements are made with difficulties. Be ready to take the devious road. And this is my experience in achieving success. In science, do not be afraid of difficulties, for it is these difficulties that need you to solve. Such is the motto of our institute.

Chapter 8
VARIATION OF TACTICS

Flexibility and change is a superb art in war and the living soul of war. There is no fixed pattern in war. The outcome of war is determined by the competition in strength and wisdom. And the core of wisdom is flexibility and change. Change, you are in an active position, otherwise in a passive position. Clinging to conventions will invite attack.

Sun Tzu said: Generally, in war, the general receives his commands from the sovereign, assembles troops and mobilizes the people. When on grounds hard of access, do not encamp[1]. On grounds intersected with highways, join hands with your allies[2]. Do not linger on critical ground[3]. In encircled ground, resort to stratagem[4]. In desperate ground[5], fight a last-ditch battle. There are some roads which must not be followed[6], some troops which must not be attacked, some cities which must not be assaulted, some ground which must not be contested, and some commands of the sovereign which must not be obeyed. Hence, the general who thoroughly understands the advantages that accompany variation of tactics knows how to employ troops[7]. The general who does not is unable to use the terrain to his advantage[8] even though he is well acquainted with it. In employing the troops for attack, the general who does not understand the variation of tactics, even if he is familiar with the Five Advantages[9], will be unable to use them effectively[10].

And for this reason, a wise general in his deliberations must consider both favorable and unfavorable factors[11]. By taking into account the favorable factors, he makes his plan feasible[12]; by taking into account the unfavorable, he may avoid possible disasters[13].

What can subdue the hostile neighboring rulers is to hit what hurts them most[14]; what can keep them constantly occupied is to make trouble for them[15]; and what can make them rush about is to offer them ostensible allurements[16].

It is a doctrine of war that we must not rely on the likelihood of the enemy not coming, but our own readiness to meet him[17]; not on the chance of his not attacking, but on the fact that we have made our position invincible[18].

There are five dangerous faults which may affect a general: if reckless, he can be killed; if cowardly, captured[19]; if quick-tempered, he can be provoked to rage and make a fool of himself[20]; if he has too delicate a sense of honor, he is liable to fall into a trap because of an insult[21]; if he is of a compassionate nature, he may get bothered and upset[22]. These are the five serious faults of a general, ruinous to the conduct of war. The ruin of the army and the death of the general are inevitable results of these five dangerous faults. They must be deeply pondered.

8.1 Notes

1. When on grounds hard of access, do not encamp: "ground hard of access" means place that is difficult to pass.

2. On grounds intersected with highways, join hands with your allies: "grounds intersected with highways" means places that are convenient in transportation. "join hands with your allies" means to ally yourself with neighboring countries as your backup.

3. Do not linger on critical ground: quickly pass the dangerous place.

4. In encircled ground, resort to stratagem: in a place that is easy to be besieged, plan a strategy to get rid of the trouble.

5. Desperate ground: a place that one cannot survive unless fights a last-ditch battle.

6. There are some roads which must not be followed: do not follow some roads.

7. Hence, the general who thoroughly understands the advantages that accompany variation of tactics knows how to employ troops: if the general has a good knowledge of the advantages and disadvantages of all kinds of terrain and of how to deal with it, he knows how to operate troops in war.

8. The general who does not is unable to use the terrain to his advantage even though he is well acquainted with it: if the general does not thoroughly understand the advantages of the variation of tactics, he cannot benefit from terrain even if he knows the terrain.

9. Five Advantages: There are some roads which must not be followed, some troops which must not be attacked, some cities which must not be assaulted, some ground which must not be contested, and some commands of the sovereign which must not be obeyed.

10. Will be unable to use them effectively: cannot give full play to the troops' fighting capacity.

11. Must consider both favorable and unfavorable factors: must give full consideration to the advantages and disadvantages.

12. By taking into account the favorable factors, he makes his plan feasible: if one has considered the advantage of it, the fighting task can be finished.

13. By taking into account the unfavorable, he may avoid possible disasters: if one has considered the disadvantage when seeing the advantage, the possible disasters can be avoided.

14. What can subdue the hostile neighboring rulers is to hit what hurts them most: use what the enemy hates to hurt him in order to subdue him.

15. What can keep them constantly occupied is to make trouble for them: use dangerous things to bother the enemy so that he might be at a loss how to handle the case.

16. And what can make them rush about is to offer them ostensible allurements: offer the enemy small bait to make them rush around.

17. We must not rely on the likelihood of the enemy not coming, but our own readiness to meet him: do not expect that the enemy will not come, but rely on ourselves to be ready for his coming.

18. Not on the chance of his not attacking, but on the fact that we have made our position invincible: do not expect that the enemy will not attack, but rely on our great strength that can deter the enemy from attacking.

19. If cowardly, captured: if the generally is mortally afraid of death, it

is very likely that he will be captured.

20. If quick-tempered, he can be provoked to rage and make a fool of himself: if the general is quick-tempered and reckless, he might fall in the trap to be scorned by the enemy.

21. If he has too delicate a sense of honor, he is liable to fall into a trap because of an insult: if the general pays too much attention to his moral integrity and reputation, he might fall into the enemy's trap because of an insult.

22. If he is of a compassionate nature, he may get bothered and upset: if the general loves his people too much without weighing up the pros and cons and having a general view of the situation, he is likely to be bothered and upset.

8.2 Explanation

Sun Tzu said that normally in war, the general receives orders from the sovereign and then organizes the troops to confront the enemy on the battlefield. When the troops come across grounds that are hard to pass such as mountains, forests, hazardous defiles, marshes and swamps, do not encamp there. When arriving at a place which is on the junction of several countries and convenient in traffic, establish a good relationship with you neighboring countries. When on a critical ground where there is hardly provisions and thus hard to survive, do not linger on. When running to an encircled place where the roads are narrow and the terrain is difficult, make a strategy to defeat the enemy. When landed in a desperate ground where there is no road before while there is chasing enemy behind, fight a last-ditch battle. There are some roads that though can be passed yet we must not follow. There are some enemies that though they can be attacked yet we must not attack. There are some cities that can be assaulted yet we must not assault. There are some lands that though can be contended for we must not contend for. And there are some orders that though are given by the sovereign yet we must not obey if the circumstance is not appropriate.

Therefore, if the general knows the advantages and disadvantages of using different tactics according to different circumstances, he really knows how to employ troops. Otherwise, even though he is familiar with the terrain, he cannot use the terrain to his advantage. In operating troops in war, if the general does not know the variation of tactics, even if he understands the advantages and disadvantages of the five terrains (grounds hard of access, rounds intersected with highways, critical ground, encircled ground, desperate ground,), he is not able to mobilize all the favorable factors of the troops.

Thus, a wise general should take into account both the favorable and unfavorable factors in his deliberations. In this way, his plan of battle can go on wheels. Under favorable conditions, by giving full consideration to unfavorable factors, he can pre-exclude all possible disasters.

If one wants to check the neighboring countries from expanding, he must use all kinds of means to hurt them. If one wants the neighboring countries to be driven at his will, he has to produce various troubles to keep them busy. If one wants the neighboring countries to be used at his will, he has to offer various baits to lure them.

Thus, the general principle of operating troops is that do not rely on the likelihood of the enemy not coming, but on our own readiness for his coming. Do not rely on the chance of his not attacking, but on our own invincible defense.

So there are five fatal faults which may bring disaster to a general: if fighting recklessly, he can be killed; if mortally afraid of death, he can be captured; if quick-tempered, he can be provoked to rage and make a fool of himself; if he pays too much attention to his honor and integrity, he is liable to fall into a trap because of an insult; if he loves his people too much, he may get bothered and upset. These are the five serious faults of a general that are disasters to the operation of troops. The defeat of the entire army and the death of the general are both results of these five dangerous faults. Therefore, they deserve much attention and deep thought.

8.3 Analysis

Though short in length, this chapter is profound in thought, beautiful in words and full of philosophy. It is both inspiring and has reference value to the management of troops, country and business.

Its main idea is that variation of tactics is a must in conduction war. "Nine" in Chinese means many. It is the limit of digit. Variation of tactics is the living soul of war.

It is a bold idea that the general cannot obey the commander of the

115

sovereign when he is on the battle field. It is a thought that emphasizes practically solving problems according to actual conditions to keep the situation on the battle field from being influenced by outside interference. On the battlefield, the commander should be endowed with more rights to make his own decisions. There are five faults of a general that may land him in danger: if reckless, he can be killed; if cowardly, captured; if quick-tempered, he can be provoked to rage and make a fool of himself; if he has too delicate a sense of honor, he is liable to fall into a trap because of an insult; if he is of a compassionate nature, he may get bothered and upset. A general should pay much attention to prevent himself from committing these faults. This is a valuable experience summarized in war and deserves the general's attention. Change leads survival while invariability results in defeat. A true success can turn an impasse into a way out and desperation into hope. The human world is complex and everything in it cannot be without change. One change brings access, three changes leads to survival and many changes makes success. And this is the essence in variation of tactics.

There is no fixed pattern in war. Its outcome is determined by the competition in strength and wisdom. And the core of wisdom is variation of tactics. Change, you are in an active position, otherwise in a passive position. Those who cling to conventions are always defeated by those who are good masters of variations of tactics.

Another brilliant idea in this chapter is to be ready at all times to defeat the enemy coming to attack.

Besides, the idea of "divide one into two" is raised in this chapter. As advantage and disadvantage can transform into each other, one should see the unfavorable side as well as the favorable one.

When in adversity, we should see the bright side and when in prosperity, we should be prepared for danger.

It also proposes that every excellent commander and entrepreneur should get rid of personal bad habits and form good ones by elevating his mind, which only brings benefits to troops and enterprises.

8.4 Cases

Case 1

The idea of "precautions avert perils" proposed by Sun Tzu is valuable experience in military war and business. We have to rely on our great strength, exploit our strengths and avoid weaknesses to awe the enemy and deter him from attacking. Even if the enemy attacks us, we have enough power to defeat them for we have set precautions.

As to business, if one can make good use of the idea of "precautions avert perils," he can always turn ill luck into good and reduce the risk.

In Japan where the competition is so fierce, Honda Motor Corporation always manages to survive in a desperate situation. "Is this all due to good luck?" A famous economist asked Soichiro Honda.

Honda responded: "Our good luck is the Honda-style crisis management."

In the world's auto industry, there is a Honda car in every eighty cars. In America, the world's largest car market, 6.3 million cars were sold in 1992, among which one fourth were from Honda. But what is most attractive about Honda is its motorcycle. In auto industry, Honda Motor Company ranks the third in Japan, even far behind jumbos such as "General Motor," "Ford," and "Benz" in the world. But in motor industry, it is not only the big boss in Japan but also second to none in the world. In 1991, Honda Motor Company produced over 1.34 million motorcycles, among which 518,000 were exported. Motorcycles branded with HONDA run all over the world.

In 1970s when Honda motorcycles were in vogue, General Manager Soichiro Honda suddenly put forward "Southeast Asia Business Strategy," proposing to develop the market in Southeast Asia.

At that time, the battlefield for the competition of motorcycles is European and American markets. While the economy in Southeast Asia only started and the living standard there was relatively low. Motorcycles were high-end consumer goods there that people gave a wide berth to. Most people in Honda felt puzzled about his proposal.

After full consideration, Soichiro Honda presented a detailed investigation report to explain: "American economy is going into a new round of recession so the ebb in the motor market there is coming. If we only focus on the US market, then we will suffer great losses when anything unfavorable happens to US economy. On the contrary, the economy in Southeast Asia is taking off. The motor market can form when the income per capita there is 2000 US dollars. Only by taking precautions can we stay calm in face of great trouble.

A year later, the US economy really took a sudden turn and plummeted, which dealt a heavy blow to the consumer market. Products made by Honda encountered poor sales and inventories stockpiled. Hundreds of thousands of Honda motorcycles were crowded in the garage. However, as a god sent opportunity, motorcycles began to be salable in the Southeast Asian market. Therefore, Honda repacked the products stocked in the garage according to the demands of the Southeast Asian market and sold them to Southeast Asia.

As Honda had started its publicity work one year earlier in Southeast Asia, once Honda motorcycles were launched in Southeast Asian market, they were sold well. In that year, compared with other enterprises that had suffered great losses, Honda not only did not suffer the smallest loss but also had a great performance in its sales

Since then, Honda Motor Corporation has formed the business strategy of "be prepared for danger in times of safety." Whenever the sale of a product culminates in a market, they start to develop a new generation of product and to open up a new market, so that Honda Company always has a way out in face of challenge.

Case 2

Established in 1984, Haier was the product of China's reform and was instrumental in opening up its borders. In the tide of reform and opening up, Haier started its step on the road of sustainable innovation and development by introducing advanced technology from Germany. The then insolvent small collective factory of only 600 employees has grown up into an international group of 60,000 employees with an operating income of 18.2 billion US dollars in 2009. In the market of China, Haier is not only the home appliance of the largest size. Its brand value ranks top on the list of "China's Most Valuable Brands" for the 8th straight year. Haier has set up 29 production bases, 8 comprehensive research and development centers and 19 overseas trading companies. Its network of marketing, R&D and production is spread in the global markets such as China, US, Italy and Thailand. According to Euromonitor's statistics, Haier ranked top of the global white goods.

The core of the variation of tactics is flexibility and change. It is with the strategic thought of winning among changes that Haier Group has become stronger and stronger. In summary, the different tactics Haier has adopted includes the following:

Pay Close Attention To Quality

In 1985, as that some of the staff in Haier neglected the quality of the products, 76 refrigerators had flaws. Product quality is the life of an enterprise. Defective products mean that the credibility of the enterprise has completely lost in the eyes of consumers. Therefore, its CEO Zhang Ruimin held a waste exhibition and called up all the staff to discuss how to deal with the 76 sub-quality products. At the meeting, the staff freely expressed their different opinions and in the end Zhang Ruimin ordered that the person directly in charge smash the 76 defective refrigerators with hammers, which stunned the over one thousand employees. The hammers had not only smashed the detective refrigerators but also the poor mentality of Haier people. It awakened everyone's awareness of quality. This even caused a strong shock among its employees and from then on led Haier people on the correct road of quality management. The strategic thought of starting up with quality and developing by brand has taken root in Haier people. In the national refrigerator appraisal in 1988, Haier, then only a four-year-old company, won the first gold medal in China's history of refrigerator with the highest score. Later, it also won "National Quality Management Award" and "Golden Horse Prize of Top Ten Excellent Enterprise Management." Haier products have yielded exceptionally brilliant results in the international market and are favored by users. Haier is a banner of quality.

New Concept Of Culture

In the process of reform and opening- up, Haier had already started to build its own corporate culture and exceptional innovative idea when other enterprises were still busy with establishing and maintaining their corporate images with administrative management and economy means.

In the initial stage of starting up, the enterprise spirit of Haier is selflessly dedication and seeking eminence. The management strategy laid out around this spirit is high standard, fining and zero defects. The quality strategy is that quality is the eternal theme of an enterprise. The production strategy is to pursue No. 1 and the marketing strategy is to produce one generation, research and develop one generation and conceive one generation. This series of cultural strategies have formed the rigorous Haier cultural network, reflecting the strategic aim of the whole culture of Haier and fully promoting its corporate spirit.

Now, when you walk into the central building of its headquarters, the first thing you will see is sixteen Chinese characters that summarize Haier spirit and style. It shows Haier's strong corporate spirit and concept of culture.

Innovation Value

The scientific outlook on development is the guide and innovation is the inexhaustible source of enterprise development. Every year, Haier Group launches products that can guide the market. For instance, the 3D refrigerators produced by Haier have really become a mainstream brand in the international mainstream channel. It is the only refrigerator that has been recognized by the whole world. In Europe, it has won "Red Dot Design Award," one of the world's famous three design awards. In Germany, it has won the famous PIUS X award. In the US, it has won "Best Product Design Award" by American authorities. And in China, it has won "2008 Best Product Design Award." Besides, its French door refrigerators have already become the trend-setter. In the US CES exhibition in 2010, Haier launched a tailless television with no cables, no power cords, no signal lines and no wires. Once launched, it had caused a sensation in the world. These products not only have brought new vigor to Haier but more importantly, they have created user demand and set the trend of the industry. The management innovation and product innovation have created new opportunities for the development of Haier.

New Image

The General Manager and CEO of Haier Mr. Zhang Ruimin said that: "it is through work rather than examination that our enterprise and products have developed." It is through hard work, down-to-earth work and skillful work that Haier people have successfully promoted the products in the world and established a brand-new corporate image of "sincere forever" in the eyes of consumers. In the past the twenty six years since it was set up, under the guidance of Zhang Ruimin's idea of "sincere forever," Haier Group has been active in assuming social responsibility and dedicating to the programs for public good, reward the society with true love. According to incomplete statistics, the capital and goods Haier Group used in the programs for public good is worth over RMB 500m.

Haier Group pays special attention to children and education. When Haier started to reward the society, it dedicated itself in the education of children. It has produced the scientific and education children's cartoon *Haier Brothers* of 212 episodes. So far, it has donated to build 129 Hope Primary School, a reflection of the dedication of all Haier people to the society.

Haier Groups is the world's only white home appliance sponsor in 2008 Beijing Olympics. In response to the demand of the Olympics and bearing in mind the idea of "Green Olympics and High-tech Olympics," it developed a series of "green Olympics products" and provided green home appliances to 2008 Beijing Olympics. All the parts of the products from design, development, and production are green. During the Olympics, Haier has provide 60 thousand green, energy-saving, and innovative product solutions to 37 Olympic competition venues such as the Olympic Village, the National Stadium, the Water Cube and Qingdao Olympic Sailing Center. It has also set up a Haier Service Center opposite to the Bird Nestle. It had selected 200 Haier gold service engineers to form an elite team of Olympic volunteers, maintaining, tracking and monitoring the Haier home appliances in the Olympic venues to ensure zero downtime of these home appliances.

In the trend of developing circular economy, Haier applies itself to being the advocator and explorer of the harmonious green consumer relationship between customers and the society, practicing the strategic management pattern of "green design, green production, green marketing and green recycling," providing solutions to greenhouses to the society and users, and becoming a service provider of better human residences.

New Relationship Between Leaders And Employees

In an era of internet, the fragmentation of marketing requires the enterprise to meet the consumers' individual demands. The original large-scale manufacturing has to change into the pattern of large-scale customization, i.e. to change from producing products first and then seeking customers to seeking customers first and then producing products. In this setting, the traditional pattern of "produce-stock-sell" has to turn into the user-driven pattern of "instant demand and instant supply." The commercial pattern Haier explores to create customers in an era of internet is the win-win pattern of "the unity between man and order."

In ordinary enterprises, the organizational structure is "triangle," i.e. the leaders on top and then all levels of organization and at the base the employees. While Haier has taken it upside down, turning it into "inverted triangle," i.e. the first line managers are at the top of the inverted triangle to face the customers, changing from order-givers to source-providers. Now, all the managers and employees receive commands from the users with the market as the command center.

New Concept Of Talent

Haier Group is the product of reform and expansion. There was no college graduate in Haier's predecessor Qingdao Refrigerator Factory in 1984. Under such circumstances, its CEO Zhang Ruimin put forward the idea of "everybody is a talent" and "finding talent through race," encouraging its employees to make innovations on their own positions. Any employee who could improve the efficiency and quality through small reform on his own position, the company would name this new approach or innovative tool with his name

In 1990s, demand fell short of supply in China's home appliance industry. But at that time, Haier succeeded in merging eighteen enterprises running in the red and turned them around without injecting any capital. One important thing behind this great success is its talent strategy. CEO Zhang Ruimin adheres to the idea of "trust the person in position." In the age when planned economy was switching to market economy and when the mechanism of promoting in order of seniority was still popular, trust had become the sufficient reason for its young leaders' loyalty and selfless dedication to the enterprise.

In 2000, a period of economic globalization, when ordinary enterprises were honored to have more doctors, Haier believed that "the world is our human resources," stuck to market orientation and drove innovation with users' demands. As long as the users' demands can be met, any talent and technology can be used. Haier's open-minded attitude towards human resources had attracted first-rate talents from many excellent enterprises like Cisco, Intel and Microsoft to take part in the research projects of scientific innovation in Haier.

In the age of Internet, Haier explores the organizational innovation of "independent operation." Talents are no longer the employees of the enterprise but its partners. The innovative pattern of "unity of man and order" Haier explores has drawn attention and recognition from scholars in management from Europe of the US. In the win-win pattern of "unity of man and order," "man" refers to the employee, "order" is the value created for users, that is the employee and the value created for users are united together. While win-win is that the employee can share the fruits while creating value for users. The win-win pattern of "unity of man and order" is to reflect the employee's value through their hard work to create values for users.

Concept Of After-Sale Service

The endless of demands from the users are the continuous motivation of strength of Haier. Since it was set up twenty six years ago, the users' demands are ever changing, yet Haier has been dealing with these changing demands with various tactics.

Nowadays, the traditional economy is switching to an internet economy. Users can select whatever they want in the world from the internet. This presents both challenges and presents opportunities, for the internet has put Haier at the same starting line with other international brands.

In response to this situation, Haier carries out two transitions, i.e. transitions in business pattern and enterprise. The business pattern transits from the one in traditional economy to the win-win pattern of the unity of man and order. The transition in enterprise is to shift from manufacturing to service and from "selling products" to "selling service."

In the transition, Haier is exploring "zero-distance fusion of virtual and real" and "zero-stock instant demand and instant supply." Haier get users' demands via "virtual net" such as internet and phone internet and meet their demands via "real net" such as marketing net, logistics net and service net, thus realizing no-stock instant demand and instant supply. In the innovative business pattern, what Haier provides users is not only products but also service that can improve quality of life.

Presently, Haier has set up over 1000 community stores, 5000 county-level specialty stores, 24,000 town networks, 70,000 country-level focal points in the main cities in China and logistics and delivery terminals in more than 2,500 counties. It also has over 17,000 service outlets. This formidable marketing, logistics and service network has supported Haier to realize "selling to country, home delivery and service." As long as the users have demands, Haier will go to the users' home to provide service rather than ask the users to come to the store. This is the true competitiveness.

In part of the regions overseas, users can submit demands via internet and phone to enjoy the service.

New Means Of Public Relations

Having summed up his decades of experience in enterprise management, CEO of Haier Group Zhang Ruimin said: "All the tangible assets in the company's balance sheet cannot increase in value. What can really increase in value are human resources the intangible asset. If we can turn man power into resources rather than liabilities, the company will surely be full of vigor."

The traditional financial statement focuses on capital and puts shareholders first. While the independent operation concentrates the staff and puts the staff first. In other words, it use the mechanism of the unity of man and order to inspire the creativity of the employees to create value for users and market resources so that a win-win situation can be achieved for both the enterprise and its employees and also the high efficiency, high increase in value and high pay of the staff can be realized.

For example, there is an employee in the department of refrigerators who used to be the manager of refrigerators in the industry and trade in Shanghai. When he worked there, his wife was awaiting delivery in Tianjin. He was worried about that and therefore hoped to work somewhere near Tianjin. Soon after the managers knew this, they asked the HR department to transfer him to the industry and trade in Beijing in view of the market situation, which was deeply appreciated by the employee, who has turned his appreciation into enthusiasm for his work.

Cooperation With New Partners

Based on the win-win pattern of the unity of man and order, Haier created its core competitiveness of the fusion of virtual and real networks. All over in the world, by integrating local resources, Haier has realized the localized three-in-on operation of design, production and marketing, such as the latest developed 3D refrigerator, tailless television. It has integrated the resources of worldwide famous design team and won the favor of local consumers.

The ever-increasing improvement in the international competitiveness of Haier brand is also reflected by the fact that it can exchange resources with international magnates. Haier exchanges its resources of users in domestic markets for the international magnates' resources of users in overseas market, which is also a change in the mode of development. For instance, GE has given its power of attorney of refrigerators in China to Haier and some famous home appliance brands in Europe and Japan also allow Haier to sell their products in some regions. It is a reflection of the international competitiveness of Haier brand.

Great minds think alike. The nine changes in Haier's enterprise management share the similar principles with the variation of tactics *in The Art of War*. It can be predicted that Haier as a more powerful multinational group will surely emerge in China and shines like a jewel on the top of a mountain.

Case 3

Sun Tzu said: "The general who thoroughly understands the advantages that accompany variation of tactics knows how to employ troops. The general who does not is unable to use the terrain to his advantage even though he is well acquainted with it. In employing the troops for attack, the general who does not understand the variation of tactics, even if he is familiar with the Five Advantages, will be unable to use them effectively."

To apply the variation of tactics to enterprise management requires constant innovation and seeking changes. From our own experience, we can see that innovation is the soul of the development of an enterprise. Only by innovation can an enterprise remain in an invincible position in the fierce competition.

Our Dalian Katelin Specific Alloy Institute develops and grows from innovation. When it was first set up, there was not enough capital, equipment and factories. We were confronted with too many difficulties. In face of difficulties, one has to be willing to do anything and take any risk. All human miracles are made by work. One can make nothing if he quits every time there appears a difficulty. By exceptionally hard work and skillful work, learning from work and changing tactics in work, we have carried out four management strategies and finally climbed the four steps of technological innovation.

We have implemented talent strategy, technological innovation strategy, market development strategy and enterprise management strategy, which has elevated the enterprise by four big steps.

The first step: transform the brickyard technologically. We use specific slag-free alloy welding rod without slag to conduct anti-wear treatment of the key parts of the augers in brick-makers, which has improved its productivity seven times. The second step: conduct anti-wear treatment of quick firing discharging tower of cement kiln in cement factory with the high pressure and high temperature generated by laser rods, which has improved the productivity effect over four times and won two national patents. The third step: by using the independently innovative flame plating technology, we have solved the wear resistance problem of the surface of large fan propellers that had bothered large enterprises such as power plants, steel makers and petro companies, which has prolonged the lifespan of the fan propellers by 4 to 7 times and made contribution to the safe production of enterprise. The fourth step: conduct anti-wear treatment of the metal surface of boilers in large power plants, thermoelectricity plants and nuclear power plants, which has solved the difficult problem of abrasion in equipment in the process of generating electricity, prolonged the lifespan by more than three times, reduced the huge economic loss that the stop in production, steam and electricity had brought to the country. And thus, we have walked into the highest temple of wear resistance treatment of metal surface at home and abroad. And we have received high praise from foreign fellow experts and created direct economic benefits worth billions of yuan for the country.

Therefore, our institute has won Outstanding Contribution Award for National Development of Productivity in the Sixth Selection of National Advanced Productive Forces Theories and Practice Achievements. It fully demonstrates that only by constant innovation can an enterprise gain full speed in the development of productivity and make new and greater contribution to the building of an innovation-oriented country.

Do not be afraid of the difficulties in your work. It is these difficulties that need you to solve. Wish you every success!

-Author's note

Chapter 9
ON THE MARCH

This chapter discusses how to deploy the troops, how to observe the situation of the enemy and see the nature through the phenomenon in war. It raises the principle of directing troops that "soldiers must be treated in the first instance with humanity, but kept under control by iron discipline" which is of significant guiding value to today's management of troops, business and enterprise.

Sun Tzu said: Generally, when an army takes up a position and sizes up the enemy situation, it should pay attention to the following: When crossing the mountains, be sure to stay in the neighborhood of valleys; when encamping, select high ground facing the sunny side[1]; when high ground is occupied by the enemy, do not ascend to attack[2]. These are the principles for taking up a position in mountains. After crossing a river, you should get far away from it[3]. When an advancing invader[4] crosses a river, do not meet him in midstream. It is advantageous to allow half his force to get across and then strike[5]. If you wish to fight a battle, you should not go to meet the invader near a river which he has to cross[6]. When encamping in the riverine area, take a position on high ground facing the sun. Do not take a position at the lower reaches of the enemy[7]. This relates to positions near a river. In crossing salt marshes[8], your sole concern should be to get over them quickly, without any delay[9]. If you encounter the enemy in a salt marsh, you should take position close to grass and water with trees to your rear. This has to do with taking up a position in salt marshes. On level ground, take up an accessible position and deploy your main flanks on high grounds with the front lower than the back. This is how to take up a position on level ground. These are principles for encamping in the four situations named. By employing them, the Yellow Emperor conquered his four neighboring sovereigns[10].

Generally, in battle and maneuvering, all armies prefer high ground to low[11] and sunny places to shady[12]. If an army encamps close to water and grass with adequate supplies[13], it will be free from countless diseases and this will mean victory. When you come to hills, dikes, or embankments, occupy the sunny side, with your main flank at the back[14]. All these methods are advantageous to the army and can exploit the possibilities the ground offers[15]. When heavy rain falls in the upper reaches of a river and foaming water descends, do not ford and wait until it subsides[16]. When encountering

'Precipitous Torrents[17]', 'Heavenly Wells[18]', 'Heavenly Prison[19]', 'Heavenly Net[20]', 'Heavenly Trap[21]', and 'Heavenly Cracks[22]', you must march speedily away from them. Do not approach them. While we keep a distance from them we should draw the enemy toward them. We face them and cause the enemy to put his back to them. If in the neighborhood of your camp there are dangerous defiles[23] or ponds and low-lying ground[24] overgrown with aquatic grass and reeds[25], or forested mountains with dense tangled undergrowth, they must be thoroughly searched[26], for these are possible places where ambushes are laid and spies are hidden[27].

When the enemy is close at hand and remains quiet, he is relying on a favorable position. When he challenges battle from afar, he wishes to lure you to advance. When he is on easy ground, he must be in and advantageous position[28]. When the trees are seen to move, it means the enemy is advancing; when many screens have been placed in the undergrowth, it is for the purpose of deception[29]. The rising of birds in their flight is the sign of an ambuscade. Startled beasts indicate that a sudden attack is forth-coming[30]. Dust spurting upwards in high straight columns indicates the approach of chariots[31]. When it hangs low and is widespread, it betokens that infantry is approaching[32]. When it branches out in different directions, it shows that parties have been sent out to collect firewood[33]. A few clouds of dust moving to and fro signify that the army is camping[34]. When the enemy's envoys speak in humble terms, but the army continues preparation, it means it will advance[35]. When their language is strong and the enemy pretentiously drives forward, these may be signs that he will retreat[36]. When light chariots first go out and take positions on the wings, it is a sign that the enemy is forming for battle[37]. When the enemy is not in dire straits but asks for a truce, he must be plotting[38]. When his troops march speedily and parade in formations, he is expecting to fight a decisive battle on a fixed date[39]. When half his forces advances and half retreats, he is attempting to decoy you. When his troops lean on their weapons, they are famished. When drawers of water drink before carrying it to camp, his troops are suffering from thirst. When the enemy sees an advantage but does not advance to seize it, he is fatigued. When birds gather above his camp sites, they are unoccupied. When at night the enemy's camp is clamorous, it betokens nervousness. If there is disturbance in the camp, the general's authority is weak. If the banners and flags are shifted about, sedition is afoot. If the officers are angry, it means that men are weary. When the enemy feeds his horses with grain, kills the beasts of burden for food[40] and packs up the utensils[41] used for drawing water, he shows no intention to return to his tents and is determined to fight to the death. When the general speaks in meek[42] and subservient tone to his subordinates[43], he

128

has lost the support of his men. Too frequent rewards indicate that the general is at the end of his resources[44]; too frequent punishments indicate that he is in dire distress[45]. If the officers at first treat the men violently and later are fearful of them[46], it shows supreme lack of intelligence. When envoys are sent with compliments in their mouths, it is a sign that the enemy wishes for a truce. When the enemy's troops march up angrily and remain facing yours for a long time, neither joining battle nor withdrawing, it demands great vigilance and thorough investigation.

In war, numbers along confer no advantage[47]. If one does not advance by force recklessly[48], and is able to concentrate his military power through a correct assessment of the enemy situation and enjoys full support of his men, it would suffice[49]. He who lacks foresight and underestimates his enemy[50] will surely be captured by him.

If troops are punished before they have grown attached to you, they will be disobedient[51]. If not obedient, it is difficult to deploy them. If troops have become attached to you, but discipline is not enforced, you cannot employ them either. Thus, soldiers must be treated in the first instance with humanity, but kept under control by iron discipline[52]. In this way, the allegiance of soldiers is assured. If orders are consistently carried out and the troops are strictly supervised[53], they will be obedient. If orders are never carried out, they will be disobedient. And the smooth implementation of orders reflects harmonious relationship between the commander and his troops[54].

9.1 Notes

1. When encamping, select high ground facing the sunny side: pitch the army on a high ground that faces the sun.

2. When high ground is occupied by the enemy, do not ascend to attack: when the enemy has taken up the high ground, do not attack it from below.

3. After crossing a river, you should get far away from it: after crossing a river, pitch the troops far away from the river.

4. Advancing invader: the enemy.

5. It is advantageous to allow half his force to get across and then strike: Do not attack the enemy when he has just arrived at the

water side. Attack him when he is half in the water, for at that time, the formation of his troops is in disorder and thus is vulnerable to attack.

6. You should not go to meet the invader near a river which he has to cross: do not attack the invading enemy beside the river.

7. Do not take a position at the lower reaches of the enemy: do not encamp your army at the lower reaches of the river, in case the enemy will cut off the water or poison the water.

8. In crossing salt marshes: when you are crossing the salt marshes.

9. Your sole concern should be to get over them quickly, without any delay: once you come across the salt marshes, you should get over it quickly and never stay there and encamp.

10. The Yellow Emperor conquered his four neighboring sovereigns: this is the reason why the Yellow Emperor can defeat the leaders of his neighboring tribes. The Yellow Emperor is the legendary ancestor of Han, leader of a tribal alliance. It is said that he had defeated Yan Emperor at Banquan, killed Chiyou at Zhuolu, and expelled Xunyu in the north, and thus united the Yellow River Valley.

11. Prefer high ground to low: like the high ground while hate the low one.

12. (Prefer) sunny places to shady: value the sunny places while despising the shady ones.

13. If an army encamps close to water and grass with adequate supplies: the army should encamp in a place where there is water, grass, and sufficient supplies.

14. Occupy the sunny side, with your main flank at the back: encamp the troops on the sunny side and the main flank against the high ground.

15. Exploit the possibilities the ground offers: benefit from the terrain.

16. When heavy rain falls in the upper reaches of a river and foaming

water descends, do not ford and wait until it subsides: when it rains in the upper reaches of a river and foaming water comes, do not cross the river until it calms.

17. Precipitous Torrents: perilous terrain with cliffs on both sides and water flowing in between.

18. Heavenly Wells: terrain with cliffs on four sides and low ground in the center.

19. Heavenly Prison: terrain that is surrounded by steep precipices and is easy to get in but hard to get out.

20. Heavenly Net: a place overgrown with thistles and thorns. Once the army gets in, it is hard to get hard as if were in a net.

21. Heavenly Trap: low-lying and muddy place that is easy to be trapped.

22. Heavenly Cracks: narrow valley between two mountains that is difficult of access.

23. If in the neighborhood of your camp there are dangerous defiles: dangerous defiles are places that are denied by steep precipices and mountains.

24. Ponds and low-lying ground overgrown with aquatic grass: low-lying places that are filled with water.

25. Reeds: places overgrown with aquatic weeds.

26. They must be thoroughly searched: one must search it carefully and repeatedly.

27. These are possible places where ambushes are laid and spies are hidden: these are the places where ambushes are most likely to lay and spies to hide.

28. When he is on easy ground, he must be in and advantageous position: the reason why the enemy encamps on the flat ground is that it is easy to advance and withdraw.

29. When many screens have been placed in the undergrowth, it is for the purpose of deception: the enemy sets too many obstacles in the undergrowth to puzzle us.

30. Startled beasts indicate that a sudden attack is forth-coming: if you see beasts are startled to run, it means the enemy is carry out attack on a large scale.

31. Dust spurting upwards in high straight columns indicates the approach of chariots: if you see the dust soars upwards in high straight columns, it means that the enemy's chariots are coming.

32. When it hangs low and is widespread, it betokens that infantry is approaching: if the dust roars low and wide, it means the enemy's infantry is coming.

33. When it branches out in different directions, it shows that parties have been sent out to collect firewood: if the dust spreads in order on and off, it means that the enemy is cutting down trees.

34. A few clouds of dust moving to and fro signify that the army is camping: if the dust is scarce yet constantly rises, it means the enemy is investigating the terrain and ready to encamp.

35. When the enemy's envoys speak in humble terms, but the army continues preparation, it means it will advance: if the envoy sent by the enemy speaks humbly yet the army continues its war readiness, it means the enemy is going to attack.

36. When their language is strong and the enemy pretentiously drives forward, these may be signs that he will retreat: if the envoy sent by the enemy speaks in strong terms yet the army pretends to forge forward, it means the enemy is going to withdraw.

37. When light chariots first go out and take positions on the wings, it is a sign that the enemy is forming for battle: If the enemy set the light chariots on its flanks, it means he is laying out the formation for the battle.

38. When the enemy is not in dire straits but asks for a truce, he must be plotting: if the enemy sends an envoy to ask for a truce without being in trouble, there must be schemes.

39. When his troops march speedily and parade in formations, he is expecting to fight a decisive battle on a fixed date: if the enemy marches fast and lays out formation, it means he is ready to fight.

40. When the enemy feeds his horses with grain, kills the beasts of burden for food: feed the horses with grain and kill the beasts for meat.

41. Packs up the utensils: the enemy has packed up the utensils.

42. Meek: gentle.

43. (When the general speaks in meek and) subservient tone to his subordinates: (the general) talks to the soldiers gently.

44. Too frequent rewards indicate that the general is at the end of his resources: if the enemy rewards his soldiers time and time again, it means he is in plight.

45. Too frequent punishments indicate that he is in dire distress: if the enemy punishes the soldiers too many times, it means he is already in trouble.

46. If the officers at first treat the men violently and later are fearful of them: the general treats the soldiers badly at first and then fears them.

47. Numbers along confer no advantage: more soldiers does not necessarily mean better.

48. If one does not advance by force recklessly: as long as one does not rashly attack.

49. Is able to concentrate his military power through a correct assessment of the enemy situation and enjoys full support of his men, it would suffice: it would be enough if (one can) concentrate his military strength, correctly assess the enemy's situation and win support from the soldiers.

50. Lacks foresight and underestimates his enemy: has no foresight and despises the enemy for no good reason.

51. If troops are punished before they have grown attached to you, they will be disobedient: if the general punish the soldiers before they have become attached to him, they will bear resentment against him.

52. Thus, soldier must be treated in the first instance with humanity, but kept under control by iron discipline: (the general) should educate the soldiers with politics and moral principles and unite and rectify the troops with military law and discipline.

53. If orders are consistently carried out and the troops are strictly supervised: if the troops are strictly disciplined to carry out orders.

54. And the smooth implementation of orders reflects harmonious relationship between the commander and his troops: the reason why orders can be smoothly carried out is that the general and the soldiers get along and trust each other.

9.2 Explanation

Sun Tzu said that when an army marches, encamps, lays out strategies, sizes up and assesses the enemy's situation, it should pay attention to the following things: When crossing the mountains, march along the valleys grown with aquatic weeds; encamp on the high ground facing the sunny side with a broad view; and do not attack from below the high ground occupied by the enemy. This is the principle of deploying troops in mountains. After crossing a river, encamp far away from it. When the enemy crosses a river to attack us, do not strike him when he is just in water. It is ideal to attack when his troops are half in the river. If you wish to fight a decisive battle with the enemy, do not lay out the formation near the river. When encamping, take a position on high ground facing the sun and do not encamp at the lower reaches of the enemy. This is the principle of deploying troops near a river. When you are crossing salt marshes, get over them quickly without any delay. If you encounter the enemy in a salt marsh, take a position close to grass and water with trees to your rear. This is the principle of deploying troops in salt marshes. If you are on the plain, take up an open place and deploy your main flanks on high grounds with flat ground in front, steep precipices at back and the front lower that the back. This is the principle of deploying troops on the plain. It is by applying the above four principles that the Yellow Emperor has successfully defeated his four neighboring sovereigns.

Generally, all armies prefer dry high ground to low wet ones, value sunny places and dislike shady ones. If an army encamps close to a place with rich aquatic grass and sufficient supplies, it will be free from countless diseases and this will guarantee victory. When you come to hills, dikes, or embankments, occupy the sunny side, with your main flanks at the back. All these methods advantageous to the army are based on the topographic conditions. When heavy rain falls in the upper reaches of a river and foaming water descends, you should not cross the river till it subsides. When coming across "Precipitous Torrents", "Heavenly Wells", "Heavenly Prison", "Heavenly Net", "Heavenly Trap", and "Heavenly Cracks", you must stay away from them and leave as fast as possible. While keeping a distance from them yourself, you should try to draw the enemy towards them. We face them and cause the enemy to put his back to them. If there are dangerous road, lakes, marshes, reeds, mountains and grounds overgrown with plants near where you march and encamp, you must search them repeatedly with great prudence, for they might be the places where the enemy has set the ambush and his spies are hiding. If the enemy gains on yet keeps quiet, it is because he relies on the favorable position difficult of access. If the enemy challenges us from afar, he wants to lure us to advance. If he intentionally encamps on flat ground, there must be benefits. If you can see the trees moving, it means the enemy is coming to attack. If there are many barriers in the undergrowth, they are deceptive trips set by the enemy. If you see rising birds, it means there is an ambush. If you see startled beasts fleeing, it means the enemy is launching a large-scale attack. If you see the dust roaring upwards in high straight columns, it means the enemy's light chariots are coming. If the dust hangs low and is widespread, it indicates the approach of the infantry. If the dust branches out in different directions, it means that the enemy is cutting firewood. And if little dust hangs on and off, it signifies that the enemy is pitching camps. If the envoy sent by the enemy speaks in humble terms, the enemy is ready to attack. If the envoy speaks in tough terms and the army pretends to attack, he is actually going to withdraw. If the enemy's chariots set out first on its flanks, he is laying out formation. If the enemy sends an envoy to ask for a truce before being thwarted, he must be plotting. If the enemy's soldiers run speedily and lineup, it means that the enemy wants to fight a decisive battle. If half his troops advances and half retreats, he is trying to lure us. If the enemy's forces lean on the weapons, they are hungry. If the soldier who fetches water drinks first, the enemy's troops are suffering from thirst. If the troops do not advance despite seeing the benefits, it indicates that the enemy is fatigued. If you see birds flocking above the enemy's camps, it means they are empty camps. If you hear screams from his troops at night, it signifies his fear. The disturbance in the camp signifies the general's weak authority. The unsteadiness of the flags and banners means the troops are in disorder. The irascibility of the officers betokens the fatigue of the entire army. If the enemy kills horses for food, it means there is no food in the army. If the utensils are packed up and no soldiers go back to the tents, it means that the enemy is trying to fight desperately to break out of encirclement. If the general speaks gently to his subordinates, it means he has lost support. If he rewards the soldiers too often, it means the enemy is at the end of resources. If he punishes the soldiers time and time again, it means the enemy is in dire distress. The general who treats his subordinates badly and then fears them is the least intelligent general. If the enemy sends an envoy to bring gifts in complimentary words, if means he wants a truce. And if the enemy's troops march up angrily yet neither advance nor retreat for a long time, you should be vigilant and observe his intention carefully.

In war, more forces does not necessarily mean better. As long as one does not advance rashly, it suffices to concentrate his forces, find out the enemy's situation and win trust and support from his subordinates. The general who lacks foresight and underestimates his enemy will surely be captured by the enemy.

If you punish the soldiers before they have grown attached to you, they will be disobedient, which will make it difficult to direct their actions. It is also difficult to command them if no discipline is enforced once they become attached to you. Thus, the general who treats his soldiers with humanity but keeps them under control by iron discipline will surely be respected and revered by his subordinates. If you discipline the soldiers to strictly carry out your orders, they will be obedient. Otherwise they will form the habit of not obeying orders. If orders are carried out smoothly, it signifies that the commander and his troops live in harmony and trust each other.

9.3 Analysis

This chapter is entitled *On the March*. Yet the march here is different from the march in modern military. It means principles of deploying troops in war. This chapter discusses how to deploy troops and how to encamp in mountains, near rivers, in salt marshes, on the plains and on other special terrains.

"All armies prefer high ground to low and sunny places to shady, encamp close to water and grass with adequate supplies." This is a scientific summary of how the ancients made use of terrain in war by Sun Tzu. Analyzing and assessing the specific situation of the enemy from his action, the changes in natural phenomena, the words of the envoy, the performance of the soldiers and the conditions of the camp. To find out the nature through phenomena is an important method for the strategists to assess the enemy's situation.

Furthermore, Sun Tzu raised the thought of managing troops of "soldier must be treated in the first instance with humanity, but kept under control by iron discipline." This thought in today is to strengthen ideological education, strictly carry out military laws, regulations and disciplines to rigorously manage troops.

Sun Tzu raised three issues in the process of commanding troops in war: encamping, sizing up the enemy situation and soldiers' attachment.

1. Encamping: discusses how to deal with the four different terrains: mountains, river, salt marshes and plain. Sun Tzu presents his opinions on how to deal with Precipitous Torrents, Heavenly Wells, Heavenly Prison, Heavenly Net, Heavenly Trap, and Heavenly Cracks.

2. Sizing up the enemy situation: Sun Tzu has provided thirty three features of the enemy's situation to help the commander with analysis and assessment. Some of them are out-of-date for there is world of difference between the past and today in weapons, equipment and talent quality. However, the thinking pattern of seeing the nature through observing various phenomena on the battlefield is worth studying, inheriting and carrying forward. Sun Tzu also said that: "In war, numbers along confer no advantage. If one does not advance by force recklessly, and is able to concentrate his military power through a correct assessment of the enemy situation and enjoys full support of his men, it would suffice." "Concentrating military power," "correctly assessing the enemy situation" and "wining full support from his men" have become military subjects for the strategists to study and practice.

3. Soldiers' attachment: Sun Tzu puts forward the principle that "soldiers must be treated in the first instance with humanity, but kept under control by iron discipline" to manage troops. This principle has already become an important part of the military canon of the strategists all over the world.

9.4 Cases

Case 1

Sun Tzu said: "Generally, when an army takes up a position and sizes up the enemy situation, it should pay attention to the following: When crossing the mountains, be sure to stay in the neighborhood of valleys; when encamping, select high ground facing the sunny side; when high ground is occupied by the enemy, do not ascend to attack. These are the principles for taking up a position in mountains."

"Sizing up the enemy situation" is to observe the enemy's situation so as to know everything about the enemy. For an enterprise, the success of its management is subject to the management of its employees.

While who is to be sized up in enterprise management? The answer is every employee in the enterprise. Our usual way is to have a heart-to-heart talk with our employees. If possible, we will eat, live and work with them to understand what they think about, their difficulties, to provide the opportunity to give full play to their specialties and try to be their psychological doctors. Only by helping them solve their misgivings and keep optimistic can we make them work enthusiastically and give full play to their potentials.

The employees from countryside always feel fidgety during the busy farming season. The whole year's work depends on a good start in spring. To plant in spring and reap in autumn are big things for the farmers. In order to solve their practical problems, we always allow them to take a short vacation during the busy farming season so that they can work whole heartedly in the institute after having helped their families with the farming work in the busy farming season.

The four ways of diagnosis in traditional Chinese medical science: observation, listening, interrogation, and pulse-taking are also applicable to the treatment of the employees. We have to care for them just as much as a doctor cares for the patients, knowing their thoughts, understanding the pulse of their thoughts, and then treating with care. The strategy of "sizing up the enemy situation" is completely suitable in enterprise management. It has to be people-oriented for the development of an enterprise depends on people. In the minds of the employees, their parents are the ones that they can rely on at home while at work the leaders are the one that they can trust, for the leaders in the institute are the most considerate ones that they can directly rely on. Just as what the employees say: every talk with the leaders of the institute teaches me about life philosophy. It is really a pleasure and an honor to talk to the academicians.

Case 2

The appropriate use of "sizing up the enemy's situation" can also bring success to business negotiation. In 1993, our country's Import and Export Company imported 2 million tons of DW products which were well received by consumers for its cheap price and high quality and therefore many factories competed with each other to get orders. By selling this product, the company had earned a lot. Despite that the delayed delivery of the product made the company miss several opportunities to attend sales exhibition and thus suffered certain economic losses, for the sake of future long-standing cooperation, the company did not file sanctions against the foreign company.

Before long, the supply of DW products fell short of demand in China. The company negotiated with the foreign company about the imports. In order to save foreign exchange for the country and reduce the purchase cost to import the product and improve its own benefits, the company required to reduce 10% of its purchase cost of the product. The company knows for sure that when the price in the international market did not change, if it asked to reduce the price at the beginning of the negotiation, the other side would hardly accept. Thus, it needed to use some negotiation skills to force the other side to give in.

After research, we had found the breakthrough and laid out a quite thorough plan for negotiation. At the beginning of the negotiation, we made good use of the delayed delivery of 2million tons of products last time. We said: "last time, your delay in delivery has caused us to miss many opportunities to take part in sales exhibition and thus suffer a great economic loss." Hearing what we said, the other side began to fidget and wasted no time explaining the delay and apologizing and then waiting in fear for our response. Seeing that the time was ripe, we clearly gave our requirement of reducing the price, hoping that the loss caused by their delay last time could be made up by the decrease in price this time. The other side could not help but accepted our requirement.

Seeing this, we proceeded to ask to increase the import number from 2 million to 5 million. Finally, the other side signed the contract. Due to the use of the tactics of "sizing up the enemy's situation," this negotiation was a great success.

Case 3

Sun Tzu said that "Thus, soldiers must be treated in the first instance with humanity, but kept under control by iron discipline. In this way, the allegiance of soldiers is assured." Our institute educates the employees with ideological education as its core and punishment as its supplement, which fully reflects the thought of human-orientation. Our institute advocates the filial piety in Chinese tradition. Filial piety is an excellent virtue in China. It is to return love. Among the 100 goodness, filial piety comes first. Therefore, our institute requires all employees to honor their parents and their elders. If one does not respect his parents, how can he have a foothold in the society?

We educate our employees to know the right things to do and make them understand that to work for the institute is to work for the country. First of all, the institute pays taxes to the country and creates a huge fortune for the country each year. In this sense, to love the institute is to love the country. In this way, the employees feel happy to work hard for the institute. They understand that to work hard for the institute is to work hard for the country and for himself, for one can have his home only when the country exists, and only when the institute gains benefits can all employees have benefits. It is this awareness that has united the thought of the institute and the employees.

A good example in case is that the employees tried to save the institute on a snowy night. On a sunny day in the winter of 2008, there was a weak northern wind and the air was dry. The institute put dozens of advanced welding rods and alloy powder in the courtyard to be dried but did not collect them at night as it was sunny. However, it suddenly snowed in the evening. Wind and snow were in order. All the employees of the institute rushed back to the factory by mere coincidence, some hailing a taxi and some running. In order to collect the welding rods and alloy powder, some carried with a pole, some pulled with carts and some carried on shoulders. Some employees did not complain even they were frozen by the cold. Very soon, all the valuable materials in the courtyard were saved, preventing the institute from suffering a loss worth over a million yuan.

The second day, the institute held a meeting to discuss how to reward the employees who had rescued the materials. The leaders thought that if they did not reward them in time, it would hurt their enthusiasm. Therefore, after deliberations, they decided to give each of them 1000 yuan and tonics worth 400 yuan as reward. When getting these, some employees could not help shedding tear. They had deeply understood the meaning of deeming the institute as home.

The thought of managing troops raised by Sun Tzu 2,500 years ago still shines in today's enterprise management. With the scientific outlook on development as the guide and by inheriting and developing the valuable cultural heritage of China, and drawing on the precious experience at all times and in over the world with great effort, our institute has won "Achievement of Chinese Management Innovation" awarded by Chinese Academy of Management Science.

Talent management strategy is the foundation of the development and success of an enterprise.

- Author's note

Chapter 10

TERRAIN

The theme of this chapter is to discuss the basic principles of making use of grounds to win victories and the methods of operating troops on different grounds. It is a penetrating treatise that first discusses military topography in the history of China. Together with The Nine Varieties of Ground, it constitutes the main content of Sun Tzu's military geography.

Sun Tzu said: Ground may be classified according to its nature as accessible[1], entangling[2], temporizing[3], constricted[4], precipitous[5] and distant[6]. Ground which both we and the enemy can traverse with equal ease is called accessible. On such ground, he who first takes high sunny positions[7], and keeps his supply routes unimpeded[8] can fight advantageously. Ground easy to reach but difficult to exit is called entangling. The nature of this ground is such that if the enemy is unprepared and you sally out, you may defeat him. But, if the enemy is prepared for your coming, and you fail to defeat him, then, returning being difficult, disadvantages will ensue. Ground equally disadvantageous for both the enemy and ourselves to enter[9] is called temporizing. The nature of this ground is such that even though the enemy should offer us the attractive bait[10], it will be advisable not to go forth but to march off[11]. When his force is halfway out because of our maneuvering[12], we can strike him with advantage. With regard to the constricted ground, if we first occupy it, we must block the narrow passes with strong garrisons[13] and wait for the enemy. Should the enemy first occupy such ground, do not attack him[14] if the pass in his hand is fully garrisoned, but only if it is weakly garrisoned. With regard to the precipitous ground, if we first occupy it, we must take a position on the sunny heights and await the enemy. If he first occupies such ground, we should march off[15] and do not attack him. When the enemy is situated at a great distance from us, and the terrain where the two armies deploy is similar[16], it is difficult to provoke battle and unprofitable to engage him. These are the principles[17] relating to six different types of ground[18]. It is the highest[19] responsibility of the general to inquire into them with the utmost care.

There are six situations that cause an army to fail. They are: flight[20], insubordination[21], fall[22], collapse[23], disorganization[24], and rout[25]. None of these disasters can be attributed to natural and geographical causes, but to the fault of the general. Terrain conditions being equal, if a force attacks one ten times its size, the result is flight. When the soldiers are strong and officers weak, the army is insubordinate. When the officers are valiant and the soldiers ineffective, the army will fall. When the higher officers[26] are angry and insubordinate, and on encountering the enemy rush to battle on their own account from a feeling of resentment[27] and the commander-in-chief is ignorant of their abilities, the result is collapse. When the general is incompetent and has little authority, when his troops are mismanaged, when the relationship between the officers and men is strained, and when the troop formations[28] are slovenly, the result is disorganization. When a general unable to estimate the enemy's strength uses a small force to engage a larger one or weak troops to strike the strong, or he fails to select shock troops[29] for the van, the result is rout. When any of these six situations exists, the army is on the road to defeat. It is the highest responsibility of the general that he examines them carefully.

Conformation of the ground is of great assistance in the military operations[30]. It is necessary for a wise general to[31] make correct assessments of the enemy's situation to create conditions leading to victory and to calculate distances and the degree of difficulty of the terrain[32]. He who knows these things and applies them to fighting[33] will definitely win. He who knows them not, and, therefore, unable to apply them, will definitely lose.

Hence, if, in the light of the prevailing situation, fighting[34] is sure to result in victory, then you may decide to fight even though the sovereign has issued an order not to engage. If fighting does not stand a good chance of victory, you need not to fight even though the sovereign has issued an order to engage. Hence, the general who advances without coveting fame and retreats without fearing disgrace, whose only purpose is to protect his people[35] and promote the best interests of his sovereign, is the precious jewel of the state.

If a general regards his men as infants, then they will march with him into the deepest valleys. He treats them as his own beloved sons and they will stand by him unto death. If, however, a general is indulgent[36] towards his men but cannot employ them, cherishes them but cannot command[37] them or inflict punishment on them[38] when they violate the regulations, then they may be compared to spoiled children[39], and are useless for any practical purpose.

If we know that our troops are capable of striking the enemy[40], but do not know that he is invulnerable to attack, our chance of victory is but half. If we know that the enemy is vulnerable to attack but do not know that our troops are incapable of striking him, our chance of victory is again but half. If we know that the enemy can be attacked and that our troops are capable of attacking him, but do not realize that the conformation of the ground makes fighting impracticable, our chance of victory is once again but half.

Therefore, when those experienced in war move, they are never bewildered[41]; when they act, they are never at a loss[42].

Thus the saying: Know the enemy and know yourself, and your victory will never be endangered[43]; know the weather and know the ground, and your victory will then be complete[44].

10.1 Notes

1. Accessible: convenient ground that can be passed.

2. Entangling: a ground that is easy to go to but hard to come back.

3. Temporizing: a ground where the enemy and us at each end of a narrow pass.

4. Constricted: a narrow passageway.

5. Precipitous: dangerous ground.

6. Distant: we are far from the enemy.

7. First takes high sunny positions: to take up the high sunny ground first.

8. Keeps his supply routes unimpeded: help to keep the road of transporting supplies unblocked.

9. Ground equally disadvantageous for both the enemy and us to enter: a ground that is hard to enter for both the enemy and ourselves.

10. Even though the enemy should offer us the attractive bait: even if the enemy lure us with advantages.

11. To march off: leave.

12. Maneuvering: make (the enemy) do

13. Block the narrow passes with strong garrisons: block means stuff here.

14. Not attack: let it be.

15. March off: leave.

16. Similar: equal in ground.

17. Six different types of ground: six varieties of ground.

18. Principles: law.

19. The highest: most.

20. Flight: it is one of the six situations that may cause an army to fail.

21. Insubordination: slack in military discipline and thus hard to command the subordinates.

22. Fall: the toughness of the general makes the soldiers coward, which leads to poor fighting capacity and finally to defeat.

23. Collapse: the general does not obey the order given by the commander in chief and rushes to battle on his own account due to resentment and the commander-in-chief is ignorant of their abilities, it will lead to defeat.

24. Disorganization: disorder.

25. Rout: be defeated.

26. Higher officer: military officer.

27. Resentment: anger, fury.

28. The troop formations: the layout of troops.

29. Select shock troops: choose the picked troops.

30. Of great assistance in the military operations: making good use of

ground helps to operate troops.

31. Calculate distances and the degree of difficulty of the terrain: calculate the difficulty and distances of the ground.

32. It is necessary for a wise general to: a wise general means the general who is of superior wisdom.

33. Applies them to fighting: make use of them in military operations.

34. Fighting: the law of war.

35. Only purpose is to protect his people: its only mission is to protect the people.

36. Indulgent: treat them well.

37. Command: educate.

38. Inflict punishment on them: punish them

39. Spoiled children: refers to the soldiers that do not observe military discipline.

40. If we know that our troops are capable of striking the enemy: if we are aware that our soldiers can strike the enemy.

41. They are never bewildered: decisive in taking military action.

42. When they act, they are never at a loss: the measures they take are infinite.

43. Victory will never be endangered: never will be defeated.

44. Your victory will then be complete: your victory will be endless and complete.

10.2 Explanation

Sun Tzu said: there are in all six different types of ground. They are: accessible, entangling, temporizing, constricted, precipitous and distant. Ground both we and the enemy can traverse is called accessible. On such ground, we have to first take up high sunny positions and keep the road of transporting supplies unblocked so that we have advantages in fighting the enemy. Ground easy to advance but difficult to withdraw is called entangling. On such ground, if the enemy is unprepared, we can sally out and be sure to defeat him. But, if he is prepared, it will be hard to defeat him and it will be difficult to retreat, thus landing ourselves in a disadvantageous position. Ground equally disadvantageous for both the enemy and ourselves to attack each other is called temporizing. On such ground, we should not fight him even if he offers bait. Instead, we should march off and attack him when he is halfway in the water. While on constricted ground, if we first reach there, we must block the narrow passes with strong garrisons and wait for the enemy's coming. Should the enemy first occupy such ground, we should not attack him if the pass is fully garrisoned. But if the pass is weakly garrisoned, we should attack the enemy fast and take the ground. On precipitous ground, if we first occupy it, we must take the high sunny position and wait for the enemy. However, if the enemy first occupies it, we should leave and do not attack him. When the enemy is far away from us, and the terrain where the two armies deploy is similar, it would be better not to provoke a battle. These are the principles of making use of different grounds. It is the general's major responsibility that deserves careful study.

There are six situations that may cause an army to fail: flight, insubordination, fall, collapse, disorganization, and rout. None of them can be ascribed to natural disasters. They are the results of the fault of the general. The situation where we attack the enemy whose forces are ten times ours on the terrain where the two armies deploy is similar is flight. The situation where the soldiers are strong and officers are weak is insubordinate. The situation where the officers are valiant while the soldiers are timid is fall. Collapse is the situation where the higher officers are angry and insubordinate, and rush to battle on their own account from a feeling of resentment on meeting the enemy while the commander-in-chief is ignorant of their abilities. Disorganization is a situation where the general has little authority and the discipline is not strictly carried out and hence slovenly troop formation. The situation where a general who fails to assess the enemy situation uses a small force to fight the enemy's larger force or weak one to strike the strong one, or he fails to select picked troops for the van is rout. The defeat caused by the above six situations are the major fault by the general and must be thoroughly examined.

To make correct use of ground is of great assistance to military operations. Assessing the enemy's situation, taking the initiative, examining the difficulty of ground and calculating the distance of the road are methods a wise general uses in operating troops. Those who know these methods and apply them to military operations will surely win victories and whose do not know them will definitely lose.

Therefore, if the objective conditions of a war show that we will surly win victories, we must fight even if the sovereign orders not to fight. If the objective conditions are unfavorable to us, we do not have to fight even if the sovereign has issued an order to engage. Thus, to advance is not to pursue fame and to retreat is not to avoid the disgrace of defeat. A general who can operate the troops to either advance or retreat only to protect his people in the interest of the sovereign is the precious jewel of the state.

If a general treats the soldiers as babies, they will stay with the general in spite of trials and tribulations. If he treats them as his own beloved sons, they will stand by him unto death. However, if he treats them well but cannot employ them, spoils them but cannot command them or punish them when they fail to observe military discipline, then they are like spoiled children and ineffective in fighting capacity.

The chance of victory is only half if you only know that your troops are capable of attacking the enemy without knowing that the enemy is vulnerable to attack. It is also the same that if you know that the enemy is vulnerable to attack with knowing that your troops are incapable of striking him. Still the same that if you know that the enemy is vulnerable to attack and that your troops are capable of attacking but no know that whether the terrain allows fight.

Hence, the one who knows how to operate troops will never be at a loss when taking actions and the actions he takes change all the time. Therefore, if you know the enemy and know yourself, your victory will never be endangered. And if you know the weather, the ground and the people, you will win victories ceaselessly.

10.3 Analysis

In this chapter, Sun Tzu classifies the grounds in military operations into six categories: accessible, entangling, temporizing, constricted, precipitous and distant. And then he puts forward how, according to the features of each ground, to deploy the troops and first occupy the terrain to turn disadvantages into advantages and turn a passive position into an active one. Sun Tzu believes that only by mastering and making use of ground can a general determine the basic principles of directing troops.

This chapter also raises six situations that may cause an army to fail: flight, insubordination, fall, collapse, disorganization, and rout. By a comprehensive analysis of these situations that will surely invites defeat, this chapter proposes that in military operation passive actions like striking the enemy whose forces are ten times ours, striking the enemy's large forces with small forces, the soldiers being strong while the general weak, the general being strong while the soldiers ineffective, rushing to battle on one's own and mismanaging the army should be avoided. It is a question that all generals should thoroughly examine and study.

Sun Tzu also talks about the relationship between the general and the soldiers in this chapter. A general has to care for and love his soldiers but should not spoil. He should be kind to them yet not indulgent towards them. He should both strict with them and love them as his beloved sons can the soldiers stay with him in spite of trials and tribulations.

A general should know both the enemy and himself, which is especially crucial in attack and terrain.

The theme of this chapter is to discuss the basic principles of making use of grounds to win victories and the methods of operating troops on different grounds. It is a penetrating treatise that first discusses military topography in the history of China. Together with The Nine Varieties of Ground, it constitutes the main content of Sun Tzu's military geography.

Sun Tzu reveals in this chapter the importance of clever use of terrain, enumerates the main types of ground and their respective features, presents the basic principles of operating troops on different grounds, and makes a dialectical analysis of the relationship between assessing the enemy situation and making use of ground. Besides, he talks about the six main reasons that may cause an army to lose in war and proposes the standard of a general's moral behavior and the general rule of managing troops. Thought valuing "terrain", he pays more attention to "people;" cherishing "assistance," he attaches greater importance to "activeness;" talking about terrain but means larger than terrain. They are both materialistic and dialectical, and subjective and objective.

It is the earliest monograph on military geography in China or even the world. It discusses the impact of object geographic environment on the outcome of war, on the basis of which it shows that the subjective fault will surely invites military loss by presenting that it is up to human to take the subjective initiative to make use of the six types and ground and that there are six situations that may cause an army to fail. "The six types of ground" are objective factors and "the six situations that may cause an army to fail" are subjective ones. While giving an appropriate assessment of the importance of terrain in military operations, Sun Tzu emphasizes the role of one's subjective initiative, believing that the only the combination of favorable objective conditions in terrain and the subjective initiative of the commander can a victory ensured in war.

10.4 Cases

Case 1

Sun Tzu said: "There are six situations that cause an army to fail. They are: flight, insubordination, fall, collapse, disorganization, and rout. None of these disasters can be attributed to natural and geographical causes, but to the fault of the general."

Sun Tzu ascribes the six situations flight, insubordination, fall, collapse, disorganization, and rout to the mismanagement of the general. There are also six situations similar to these in enterprise management which are put down to the mismanagement of the leader at the basic level for he is the key to the lower management of an enterprise.

In order to win victories in military operations, an excellent military officer has to be chosen, and in order to make more achievements, an enterprise has to select an excellent leader or director. Drawing lessons from the standard of choosing an officer in *The Art of War*, out institute choose leaders according to the following standards:

1. Have correct thought; deem the institute as home, hardworking, and make him an example to the employees.

2. Consummate skills, master all technologies, innovative, can rule out mechanical failures on his own account, is the vanguard of employees.

3. Can unite the employees, be their intimate friends, and be a good teacher to them.

4. Good at communication, clear and concise in giving tasks, and have

151

the charisma of a leader.

The above four are the standards our institute uses to choose a leader. Only by following these standards can we finish the productive task well. The key reason that we can make constant achievements is choosing leaders according to these standards, for leaders are the soul of the basic level of an enterprise and the most basic and direct link of enterprise management. They are the most important factors in enterprise management.

Case 2

Sun Tzu said: "Ground may be classified according to its nature as accessible, entangling, temporizing, constricted, precipitous and distant."

Chapter ten *Terrain* in *The Art of War* is of great guiding value to the strategic competition of our institute. Our Dalian Katelin Specific Alloy Institute is located within Dalian Jiaotong University in Liaoning Province. Dalian Jiaotong University is highly popular within Liaoning Province, which is related to the geographic location of Dalian where the university is situated. Sitting by mountains and bordering on sea with beautiful scenery, Dalian is a famous tourist city in China and also enjoys some fame in the world. It is rich in tourism resources. There is the famous Xinghai Park the swimming beach, Asia's largest Xinghai Square, Sun Asia Ocean World in Xinghai Bay, Tiger Beach Park & Pole Aquarium, Bird-Sing Woods, Dalian Forest Zoo, Shihuyuan, Golden Pebble Beach, Kingdoms of Discovery, Labor Park, Lvshun Museum, Naval Weapons Exhibition Center, Baiyu Mountain, Jiguan Mountain, Japan-Russia Prison Site, Golden Mountain, Tahe Bat, Snake Island, Changhai County, Caishen Island, River Deer Island, Sanshan Island, Bangchui Island, Anbo Hot Spring, Ski Resort and Zhuanghe Bingyugou. Pleasant in climate, Dalian is a good summer resort. Enjoying Dalian's exceptionally advantageous geographic sources, our institute invites the clients to come to Dalian to attend meetings, hold technical exchange seminars, introduce experience, conduct field investigation and visit the high-tech laboratories and factories in our institute. By doing this, our relationship with the clients becomes closer, making the clients come to realize that it helps the development of their enterprises to make friends with an institute like ours that treats its friends well, for it can be trusted at a crucial moment or even in times of difficulties. We not only have met intimate friends, but more importantly, the clients will choose our institute to have technical cooperation by comparing our technological strength, quality, and credit with others' after the field investigation.

Besides, the distance of terrain in military operations mentioned in *The Art of War* goes the same with business war. We cannot choose a distant market but rather be near one in our development of that market. Our principle in developing a market is to first grasp the local market, for we enjoy advantages in time, geographic location and support here. That the clients are near means that a huge amount of transportation expenses can be saved. If we open a market in the local place, we can save transportation expenses and travel expense and thus our cost can be reduced. If we use this part to benefit the clients, they will appreciate us for doing this yet we in fact do not pay much. It is advantageous to both the institute and the clients. This is what is called "taking the advantageous position" in the art of war, the key to victory.

Meanwhile, the institute does not give up the clients outside Dalian and tries to develop markets in other places. In order to save transportation expenses and reduce cost, we have set up representatives offices outside Dalian. If there is any market demand in other places, we use the equipment in the representative offices to develop the market, which can avoid the inconvenience and fatigue caused by long-distance transportation and can ensure to be on call if the clients need. By doing this, convenience is brought to both the institute and the clients and furthermore, the cost is reduced. This is the benefit brought to enterprise by creatively studying applying *The Art of War*.

It indeed has produced desired results by applying the theories in *The Art of War* to enterprise management and the development of productivity.

Let all the entrepreneurs cleverly combine enterprise management with the art of war. In this way, the enterprise management will surely turn from the realm of necessity into the realm of freedom, making greater contribution to the development of our national productivity.

Sun Tzu said: "Conformation of the ground is of great assistance in the military operations. It is necessary for a wise general to make correct assessments of the enemy's situation to create conditions leading to victory and to calculate distances and the degree of difficulty of the terrain. He who knows these things and applies them to fighting will definitely win."
Our institute has advantages in weather, geographic location and support. We focus on improving the product quality which in our mind is the life of an enterprise and the foundation of its development. Quality means benefits and market. Our achievements are spread all over Shandong, the three

northeastern provinces, Inner Mongolia, Hebei and Henan.

Thus, we have obtained the British quality certificate.

To hew out a successful career depends on technical innovation, being practical and realistic and following the guidance of the Communist Party. By keeping to these three principles, your success can be ensured.

-Author's note

Chapter 11
THE NINE VARIETIES OF GROUND

This chapter expounds the strategic principles of making use of nine different grounds to conduct military operations. "The different measures appropriate to the nine varieties of ground and the expediency of advance or withdrawal in accordance with circumstances and the fundamental laws of human nature are matters that must be studied carefully by a general." It is an important philosophical thinking in The Art of War.

Sun Tzu said: In respect of the employment of troops, ground may be classified as dispersive, frontier, key, open, focal, serious, difficult, encircled, and desperate. When a chieftain is fighting in his own territory, he is in dispersive ground[1]. When he has penetrated into hostile territory, but to no great distance, he is in frontier ground[2]. Ground equally advantageous for us and the enemy to occupy is key ground[3]. Ground equally accessible to both sides is open[4]. Ground contiguous to three other states is focal[5]. He who first gets control of it will gain the support of the majority of neighboring states. When an army has penetrated deep into hostile territory, leaving far behind many enemy cities and towns, it is in serious ground[6]. Mountain forests, rugged steeps, marshes, fens and all that is hard to traverse fall into the category of difficult ground[7]. Ground to which access is constricted and from which we can only retire by tortuous paths so that a small number of the enemy would suffice to crush a large body of our men is encircled ground[8]. Ground on which the army can avoid annihilation only through a desperate fight without delay is called a desperate one. And, therefore, do not fight in dispersive ground; do not stop in the frontier borderlands. Do not attack an enemy who has occupied key ground[9]; in open ground, do not allow your communication to be blocked[10]. In focal ground, form alliances with neighboring states[11]; in serious ground, gather in plunder[12]. In difficult ground, press on; in encircled ground, resort to stratagems; and desperate ground, fight courageously.

In ancient times, those described as skilled in war knew how to make it impossible for the enemy to unite his van and his rear[13], for his large and small divisions to cooperate[14], for his officers, and men to support each other[15], and for the higher and lower levels of the enemy to establish contact with each other[16]. When the enemy's forces were dispersed, they prevented him from assembling them[17]; even when assembled, they managed to throw his forces into disorder[18]. They moved forward when it was advantageous to do so; when not advantageous, they halted[19]. Should one ask: 'How do I cope with a well-ordered enemy host about to attack me?' I reply: 'seize something he cherishes and he will conform to your desires.' Speed is the essence of war[20]. Take advantage of the enemy's unpreparedness, make your way by unexpected routes[21], and attack him where he has taken no precautions.

The general principles applicable to an invading force[22] are that the deeper you penetrate into hostile territory, the greater will be the solidarity of your troops, and thus the defenders cannot overcome you[23]. Plunder fertile country[24] to supply your army with plentiful food. Pay attention to the soldiers' well-being and not fatigue them[25]. Try to keep them in high spirits and conserve their energy[26]. Keep the army moving and devise unfathomable plans. Throw your soldiers into a position whence there is no escape, and they will choose death over desertion. For if prepared to die, how can the officers and men not exert their uttermost strength to fight? In a desperate situation, they fear nothing[27]; when there is no way out, they stand firm[28].

Deep in a hostile land they are bound together[29]. If there is no help for it, they will fight hard. Thus, without waiting to be marshaled, the soldiers will be constantly vigilant[30]; without waiting to be asked, they will do your will; without restrictions, they will be faithful[31]; without giving orders, they can be trusted[32]. Prohibit superstitious practices and do away with rumors[33], then nobody will flee even facing death[34]. Our soldiers have no surplus of wealth, but it is not because they disdain riches; they have no expectation of long life, but it is not because they dislike longevity[35]. On the day the army is ordered out to battle, your soldiers may weep, those sitting up wetting their garments[36], and those lying down letting the tears run down their cheeks[37]. But throw them into a situation where there is no escape and they will display the immortal courage of Zhuan Zhu and Cao Kuei[38].

Troops directed by a skillful general are comparable to the Shuai Ran[39]. The Shuai Ran is a snake found in Mount Heng[40]. Strike at its head, and you will be attacked by its tail; strike at its tail, and you will be attacked by its head; strike its middle, and you will be attacked by both its head and tail. Should one ask: 'Can troops be made capable of such instantaneous coordination as the Shuai Ran?' I reply: 'They can.' For the men of Wu and the men of Yue are enemies, yet if they are crossing a river in the same boat and are caught by a storm, they will come to each other's assistance just as the left hand helps the right. Hence, it is not sufficient to rely upon tethering of the horses and the burying of the chariots[41]. The principle of military administration is to achieve a uniform level of courage[42]. The principle of terrain application is to make the best use of both the high and low-lying grounds[43]. Thus, a skillful general conducts his army just as if he were leading a single man, willy-nilly, by the hand.

It is the business of a general to be quiet and thus ensure depth in deliberation; impartial and upright, and thus maintain good management[44]. He should be able to mystify his officers and men by false reports and appearances, and thus keep them in total ignorance. He changes his arrangements and alters his plans in order to make others unable to see through his strategies. He shifts his campsites and undertakes marches by devious routes so as to make it impossible for other to anticipate his objective[45]. He orders his troops for a decisive battle on a fixed date and cuts off their return route, as if he kicks away the ladder behind the soldiers when they have climbed up a height[46]. When he leads his army deep into hostile territory, their momentum is trigger-released in battle[47]. He drives his men now in one direction, then in another, like a shepherd driving a flock of sheep, and no one knows where he is going. To assemble the host of his army and bring it into danger this may be termed the business of the general. The different measures appropriate to the nine varieties of ground and the expediency of advance or withdrawal in accordance with circumstances[48] and the fundamental laws of human nature are matters that must be studied carefully by a general.

Generally, when invading a hostile territory, the deeper the troops penetrate, the more cohesive they will be; penetrating only a short way causes dispersion[49]. When you leave your own country behind, and take your army across neighboring territory, you find yourself on critical ground[50]. When there are means of communication on all four sides, it is focal ground. When you penetrate deeply into a country, it is serious ground. When you penetrate but a little way, it is frontier ground. When you have the enemy's strongholds on your rear, and narrow passes in front, it is encircled ground[51]. When there is no place of refuge at all, it is desperate ground. Therefore, in dispersive ground, I would unify the determination of the army. In frontier ground, I would keep my forces closely linked. In key ground, I would hasten up my rear elements[52]. In open ground, I would pay close attention to my defense. In focal ground, I would consolidate my alliances[53]. In serious ground, I would ensure a continuous flow of provisions[54]. In difficult ground, I would press on over the road[55]. In encircled ground, I would block the points of access and egress[56]. In desperate ground, I would make it evident that there is no chance of survival[57], for it is the nature of soldiers to resist when surrounded[58], to fight hard when there is no alternative, and to follow commands implicitly when they have fallen into danger[59].

One ignorant of the designs of neighboring states cannot enter into alliance with them; if ignorant of the conditions of mountains, forests, dangerous defiles, swamps, and marshes, he cannot conduct the march of an army; if he fails to make use of native guides, he cannot gain the advantages of the ground[60]. An army does not deserve the title of the invincible Army of the Hegemonic King if its commander is ignorant of even one of these nine varieties of ground[61]. Now, when such an invincible army attacks a powerful state, it makes it impossible for the enemy to assemble his forces[62]. If overawes the enemy and prevents his allies from joining him[63]. It follows that one does not need to seek alliances with other neighboring states[64], nor is there any need to foster the power of other states[65], but only to pursue one's own strategic designs[66] to overawe his enemy. Then one can take the enemy's cities and overthrow the enemy's state[67]. Bestow rewards irrespective of customary practice and issue orders irrespective of convention, and you can command a whole army as though it were but one man. Set the troops to their tasks without revealing your designs[68]. When the task is dangerous, do not tell them its disadvantageous aspect[69]. Throw them into a perilous situation and they will survive; put them in desperate ground and they will live, for when the army is placed in such a situation, it can snatch victory from defeat[70]. Now, the key to military operations lies in cautiously studying enemy's designs[71]. Concentrate your forces in the main direction against the enemy and from a distance of a thousand miles you can kill his general. This is called the ability to achieve one's aim in an artful and ingenious manner.

Therefore, on the day the decision is made to launch war, you should close the passes, destroy the official tallies, and stop the passage of all emissaries[72]. Examine the plan closely in the temple council and make final arrangements. If the enemy leaves a door open, you must rush in[73]. Seize the place the enemy values[74] without making an appointment for battle with him[75]. Be flexible and decide your line of action according to the situation on enemy side[76]. At first, then, exhibit of coyness of a maiden until the enemy gives you an opening; afterwards be swift as a running hare, and it will be too late for the enemy to oppose you.

11.1 Notes

1. When a chieftain is fighting in his own territory, he is in dispersive ground: the ground where the chieftain can easily retreat when he is in danger when fighting with the enemy on his own land is called

dispersive land.

2. When he has penetrated into hostile territory, but to no great distance, he is in frontier ground: the region that is not far into the enemy's territory and where the troops can easily go back is called frontier ground.

3. Ground equally advantageous for us and the enemy to occupy is key ground: the region that is equally advantageous for either the enemy or us who takes it first is called key ground.

4. Ground equally accessible to both sides is open: an open ground is a place where the transportation is convenient.

5. Ground contiguous to three other states is focal: the place that can bring assistance of the neighboring states to whoever occupies it first is called focal ground.

6. When an army has penetrated deep into hostile territory, leaving far behind many enemy cities and towns, it is in serious ground: the place that is deep in the enemy's territory and that there has many enemy's cities and towns at its back is called serious ground.

7. Mountain forests, rugged steeps, marshes, fens and all that is hard to traverse fall into the category of difficult ground: a place hard to pass like mountain forests, rugged steeps, marshes and fens is called difficult ground.

8. Encircled ground: a place that the route of retreat is devious and far and where the enemy can strike us with smaller forces.

9. Do not attack an enemy who has occupied key ground: when in key ground, we should occupy it first. But if the enemy occupies it first, we must not attack him.

10. In open ground, do not allow your communication to be blocked: when in open ground, make sure that the officers and subordinates can communicate with each other and the march disposition not disrupted.

11. In focal ground, form alliances with neighboring states: when in focal ground, increase diplomatic activities to form more alliances with other states so that you can get assistance.

12. In serious ground, gather in plunder: as in the interior land of the enemy's state, it is impossible to transport supplies from our own state; we have to get military supplies from the enemy's state.

13. Impossible for the enemy to unite his van and his rear: impossible for the van and rear to support each other.

14. (Impossible) for his large and small divisions to cooperate: the main forces and squads cannot rely on each other and cooperate with each other.

15. (Impossible) for his officers, and men to support each other: the commanding officers and the soldiers cannot save each other.

16. (Impossible) for the higher and lower levels of the enemy to establish contact with each other: the organizational system of troops is disrupted and the officers and the subordinates lose contact and thus cannot assemble.

17. When the enemy's forces were dispersed, they prevented him from assembling them: the troops are too scattered to gather.

18. Even when assembled, they managed to throw his forces into disorder: though the troops can assemble, they cannot display in order.

19. They moved forward when it was advantageous to do so; when not advantageous, they halted: if it is advantageous to me, I will fight, otherwise, not.

20. Speed is the essence of war: the key to operating troops is to fight a quick battle.

21. Make your way by unexpected routes: take the path beyond the expectation of the enemy.

22. The general principles applicable to an invading force: the operation law of leaving your own state and entering another's.

23. The defenders cannot overcome you: the army fighting within his own state cannot defeat the invading army.

24. Plunder fertile country: grab the crops in the fertile fields on the enemy's territory.

25. Pay attention to the soldiers' well-being and not fatigue them: attach importance to rest and do not make them over tiered.

26. Try to keep them in high spirits and conserve their energy: keep the morale high and save fighting capacity.

27. In a desperate situation, they fear nothing: when the soldiers are in dangerous situation, they will not fear anything.

28. When there is no way out, they stand firm: when in a desperate situation, the morale of the troops is stable.

29. Deep in a hostile land they are bound together: when the troops are deep into the enemy's state, they are united.

30. Thus, without waiting to be marshaled, the soldiers will be constantly vigilant: the soldiers will become more vigilant without being disciplined.

31. Without restrictions, they will be faithful: the soldiers are united and close to each other without being restricted.

32. Without giving orders, they can be trusted: they can trust and obey the general without being given orders.

33. Prohibit superstitious practices and do away with rumors: forbid superstition and dispel misgivings and rumors.

34. Nobody will flee even facing death: they will not escape even in face of death.

35. Our soldiers have no surplus of wealth, but it is not because they disdain riches; they have no expectation of long life, but it is not because they dislike longevity: that our soldiers do not have spare money does not mean that they do hate money, that they put aside life and death does not mean that they do not want to live long.

36. Those sitting up wetting their garments: the soldiers who sit up will weep and their clothes wet in tears.

37. Those lying down letting the tears run down their cheeks: tears will be all over the cheeks of the soldiers lying down.

38. They will display the immortal courage of Zhuan Zhu and Cao Kuei: be as brave as Zhuan Zhu and Cao Kuei.

39. Shuai Ran: a snake in the ancient legend.

40. Mount Heng: the north mountain of the Five Mountains.

41. It is not sufficient to rely upon tethering of the horses and the burying of the chariots: it is unreliable to bind the horses in a row and bury to stabilize the force and to show the determination of holding the ground.

42. The principle of military administration is to achieve a uniform level of courage: the way to manage the troops is to pull the soldiers together to strike the enemy as one.

43. The principle of terrain application is to make the best use of both the high and low-lying grounds: to give full play to both the strong and the weak lies in making appropriate use of terrain.

44. Impartial and upright, and thus keep a good management: being serious and impartial and hence the good management.

45. He shifts his campsites and undertakes marches by devious routes so as to make it impossible for other to anticipate his objective: change the position to set up garrisons and take devious roads when marching so that the enemy cannot plan schemes.

46. He orders his troops for a decisive battle on a fixed date and cuts off their return route, as if he kicks away the ladder behind the soldiers when they have climbed up a height: when the commander-in-chief gives military tasks to the troops, he has to cut off their route of retreat so that they can march forward courageously as if they were climbing without a ladder.

47. When he leads his army deep into hostile territory, their momentum is trigger-released in battle: if the commander marches deep into the enemy's state with his troops, it is like the arrow sent by a crossbow that dashes forward impossible to come back.

48. The different measures appropriate to the nine varieties of ground and the expediency of advance or withdrawal in accordance with circumstances: adopt different tactics and direct the troops to advance or to retreat according to different geographic locations.

49. The deeper the troops penetrate, the more cohesive they will be; penetrating only a short way causes dispersion: when fighting on the enemy' territory, if deep into the state, the soldiers will be united, if not, they will slack.

50. When you leave your own country behind, and take your army across neighboring territory, you find yourself on critical ground: the place where you leave your own state and cross the boundary into the enemy's state to fight is called critical ground.

51. When you have the enemy's strongholds on your rear, and narrow passes in front, it is encircled ground: the place where the road before is narrow, the precipices are at the back and it is easy for the enemy to disrupt our advance and retreat is called encircled ground.

52. In key ground, I would hasten up my rear elements: when fighting on key ground, we should order the troops to march forward speedily to occupy the place the enemy must pass in their retreating.

53. In focal ground, I would consolidate my alliances: when in focal ground, we should form solid alliances with neighboring states.

54. Ensure a continuous flow of provisions: continue to supplement military provisions and guarantee supplies.

55. Press on over the road: pass quickly after entering.

56. Block the points of access and egress: block the gap so that the troops have to fight a desperate battle.

57. Make it evident that there is no chance of survival: show the enemy the determination of fighting a desperate battle.

58. Resist when surrounded: rise to resist when surrounded.

59. To follow commands implicitly when they have fallen into danger: the soldiers will obey the orders in desperate situation.

60. One ignorant of the designs of neighboring states…he cannot gain the advantages of the ground: this paragraph also appears in Chapter 7 "Maneuvering."

61. An army does not deserve the title of the invincible Army of the Hegemonic King if its commander is ignorant of even one of these nine varieties of ground: this explains the importance of knowing the nine terrains, the army whose general does not know even one of the nine terrains cannot become invincible.

62. It makes it impossible for the enemy to assemble his forces: the enemy's troops and people cannot be mobilized to assemble in time.

63. If overawes the enemy and prevents his allies from joining him: the pressure formed due to a state's strong national strength can stop the enemy from making alliances with other states.

64. It follows that one does not need to seek alliances with other neighboring states: there is no need to contend to make alliances with other states.

65. Nor is there any need to foster the power of other states: it is not necessary to raise power in other states.

66. Pursue one's own strategic designs: to realize one's own strategic intent.

67. Overthrow the enemy's state: destroy the enemy's state.

68. Set the troops to their tasks without revealing your designs: assign tasks to the soldiers without telling them your intention.

69. When the task is dangerous, do not tell them its disadvantageous aspect: when operating troops, tell them only the favorable conditions and hide from them the danger of their task, which is made to firm their faith.

70. Put them in desperate ground and they will live, for when the army is placed in such a situation, it can snatch victory from defeat: only by putting the troops in a dangerous situation can they win the victory.

71. He key to military operations lies in cautiously studying enemy's designs: when operating troops, the general has to carefully examine the enemy's intention.

72. On the day the decision is made to launch war, you should close the passes, destroy the official tallies, and stop the passage of all emissaries: when making the decision to wage a war, one has to block the strategic passes, abolish the pass permit and stop contacting the enemy's envoys.

73. If the enemy leaves a door open, you must rush in: once the enemy is negligent, seize the opportunity to attack him.

74. Seize the place the enemy values: attack the vulnerable part of the enemy first to seize the initiative.

75. Without making an appointment for battle with him: do not fix a date with the enemy to fight.

76. Be flexible and decide your line of action according to the situation

on enemy side: the principles to follow change with the enemy's situation.

11.2 Explanation

Sun Tzu said: according to the principles of operating troops, the battlefield can be classified into nine types: dispersive, frontier, key, open, focal, serious, difficult, encircled, and desperate. If the battlefield is within the state, it is called dispersive ground. If it is not deep into the enemy's state, it is called frontier ground. Ground that is of equal advantage to whoever occupy first is called key ground. Battlefield that both the enemy and we can enter is called open ground. Battlefield that borders on several states and that who occupies first can form alliances with the neighboring states first is called focal ground. Ground that is deep into the enemy's territory and has many enemy's cities and towns at its back is called serious ground. All places hard to pass such as mountain forests, rugged steeps, marshes and fens fall into the category of difficult ground. Battlefield where the access is constricted, the route of retreat is devious and far away and the enemy can strike our large forces with a small one is encircled ground.

A battlefield where the army can survive if fighting a quick battle but will be completely defeated otherwise is desperate ground. Therefore, do not engage in a battle rashly in dispersive ground; do not stop in frontier ground; do not attack the enemy in key ground; make sure the troops march in order in open ground; form alliances with neighboring states actively when in focal ground; plunder the enemy's provisions when deep in serious ground; pass quickly when in difficult ground; when in encircled ground, resort to stratagems to break out; and when in desperate ground, fight courageously and seek the chance of survival from death.

In ancient times, those are good at operating troops can make it impossible for the enemy to unite his van and his rear, for his large and small divisions to cooperate, for his officers and soldiers to support each other, and for the higher and lower levels of the enemy to establish contact with each other. When the enemy's forces are dispersed, it will be hard for them to assemble. Even if they assemble, the formation will be in disorder. In a word, if the conditions are advantageous to us, we fight, otherwise not. If one asks: "What should I do if the enemy is going to attack me with large forces in good order?" the response is that seize what is most important, most critical and advantageous to the enemy. This way, he has to be manipulated by us." What is most important in operating troops is speed. Take the road unexpected by the enemy and attack him where he takes no precautions when he is unprepared.

The general laws of fighting battles deep into the enemy's territory are that the deeper we penetrate into the enemy's territory, the greater will be the solidarity of our troops, and thus it is not easy for the enemy to defeat us. Plunder provisions from the fertile places in the enemy's territory and the entire army's supplies can be guaranteed. Pay attention to rest and not fatigue the soldiers. Keep the soldiers in high spirits and save their fighting capacity. Make use of stratagem so that the enemy cannot find out our situation. Place our troops in a desperate situation so that they have no choice but to charge forward desperately. As they fight regardless of death, how can it be the victory not guaranteed? When landed in a dangerous situation, the soldiers have no way out, therefore they will be united and careful when marching deeper into the enemy's territory and be forced to fight a desperate battle when necessary. Thus, troops in such as situation will be vigilant without being marshaled, fight to their best without being required, unite and cooperate with each other without being restricted and observe discipline without being given order. Prohibit superstitions in the army lest ominous feelings and omens should appear. Dispel the soldiers' misgivings so that they will not regret even if they lose their lives in defense of the state. That our officers and soldiers do not have spare money does not mean that they do not love money. That they do not fear death does not mean that they don't want to live long. When being given the order to engage in battle, the soldiers sitting up wet their clothes and the ones lying down let the tears run down their cheeks. If the soldiers are put in a desperate situation, they will fight as courageously as Zhuan Zhu and Cao Kuei did.

Therefore, the one who is skilled in operating troops is like "Shuai Ran," a snake in Mount Heng. If you strike its head, the tail will act to help the head and the same goes the other way round. And if you strike its body, both the head and the tail will cooperate to help the body. If one asks: "Can troops be made capable of such instantaneous coordination as the Shuai Ran?" The answer is yes. The men of Wu and the men of Yue are enemies, yet when they are crossing a river in the same boat and are caught by a storm, they will come to each other's assistance just as the left hand helps the right. Thus, it is not reliable to stabilize the troops by tying the horses and carts in formation and burying deep the wheels to display the determination to fight a desperate battle. It is through appropriate management and education that the soldiers can fight of one mind. If you want to make the best use of both the strong and the weak, you have to make a reasonable use of terrain. Therefore, the one who is good at operating troops will land his troops in a desperate situation to unite the troops as if they were one person.

A general should use his foresight to make the troops calm down and make them impartial and upright with strict military discipline. He should be able to fool the eyes and ears of the soldiers and make them ignorant of his combat plan. He should change his combat tasks and stratagems so that the enemy cannot see through them. He should shift the campsites and take devious roads to march on so that the enemy cannot find out his intention. When leading his troops to battle, he should cut off their route of retreat as taking away the ladder when climbing. When leading the soldiers deep into the enemy's territory, he should show the determination to fight a desperate battle as if he were going to trigger the crossbow to release the arrow. He should burn the boat and smash the cookers so that the soldiers have to march forward. A commander should drive his troops in now in one direction, then in another, like a shepherd driving a flock of sheep, and no one knows where he is going. He should assemble the host of his army and bring it into danger so that they will fight desperately. These are the business of a general. The different measures appropriate to the nine varieties of ground and the expediency of advance or withdrawal in accordance with circumstances and the soldiers' psychology are matters that must be studied carefully by a general.

The principle of fighting in the enemy's territory is that the deeper the troops penetrate, the more united they will be and if they penetrate only a short way, dispersion might be caused. When you leave your own state and cross the neighboring state into the enemy's territory, you find yourself on critical ground. The place where the transportation is convenient is focal ground. When you penetrate deep into a country, it is serious ground. When you penetrate but a little way, it is frontier ground. When you have the enemy's strongholds on your rear, and narrow passes in front, it is encircled ground. When there is no place of refuge at all, it is desperate ground.

Therefore, in dispersive ground, we should unify the determination of the troops. In frontier ground, we should keep my forces closely linked. In key ground, we should cut off the enemy's route of retreat quickly. In open ground, we should be cautious about our defense. In focal ground, we should consolidate my alliances with neighboring states. In serious ground, we should supplement our provisions from the enemy. In difficult ground, we should pass quickly. In encircled ground, we should block the points of access and egress. In desperate ground, we should display our determination to fight a desperate battle. Therefore, the soldiers will try to resist when besieged, fight desperately when there is no alternative and follow the command when in dangerous situation.

Thus, if we do not know the designs of neighboring states, we should not form alliances with them. If we are ignorant of the conditions of mountains, forests, dangerous defiles, swamps, and marshes, we cannot march on. If we do not have a native guide, we cannot take advantage of the ground. If ignorant of even one of these aspects, we cannot be called an invincible army. An invincible army, when attacking a powerful state, can make it impossible for the enemy to assemble his forces. If it overawes the enemy, it can prevent his allies from joining him. So we do not need to contend to form alliances with other states, neither do we need to foster our power in other states. The only thing we need to do is to carry out our plans and overawe the enemy. In this way, we can take the enemy's cities and destroy his capital.

Give rewards beyond regulations, issue orders beyond government decrees, command a whole army as if it were one man. Send the troops to tasks without revealing the designs. Send them to win victory without telling them about the possible danger. Throw them into a perilous situation so that they can turn death into survival. Place them in a dangerous situation so that they can win victories. Hence, the principle of operating troops is to fool the enemy by following his designs and concentrate our forces in on direction against the enemy. In this way we can kill his general a thousand miles away. This is called the ability to achieve one's aim in an artful and ingenious manner.

Therefore, on the day we decide to engage the enemy in war, we should close the passes, abolish the pass permits, and stop contacting the enemy's envoys. The sovereign and his officials examine the plan carefully in the temple council and make final decisions. Once the enemy leaves a door open, we must take advantage of it to rush in. Seize the vulnerable part of the enemy first and do not fix a date for battle with the enemy. The way to carry out combat plans should change in response to the change in the enemy's situation. That is why we must be as coy as a maiden at first so that the enemy will not take precautions and once we decide to take actions, we have to act as fast as a running hare so that the enemy does not have time to resist.

11.3 Analysis

This chapter expounds on how to operate troops in the enemy's territory by making use of ground. According to strategic requirements, Sun Tzu classifies battlefields into nine types of grounds: dispersive, frontier, key, open, focal, serious, difficult, encircled, and desperate. Here nine means many. He also explains how to operate troops by making use of the nine grounds. But a general has to be flexible to really maser the principles of conducting operations in these grounds.

First, we have to take what the enemy values and land him in a disadvantageous ground. By using the strategy of "luring the tiger out of his den," we force the enemy to be in a disadvantageous ground and then strike him.

Secondly, we can put our troops in desperate ground to turn passive into active. Knowing the dialectic relationship between life and death, Sun Tzu encourages soldiers to fight courageously so that they can defeat the enemy and survive themselves. He wrote: "Our soldiers have no surplus of wealth, but it is not because they disdain riches; they have no expectation of long life, but it is not because they dislike longevity. On the day the army is ordered out to battle, your soldiers may weep, those sitting up wetting their garments, and those lying down letting the tears run down their cheeks. But throw them into a situation where there is no escape and they will display the immortal courage of Zhuan Zhu and Cao Kuei."

Thirdly, we should make flexible use of grounds. We should take all kinds of factors into consideration to master it objectively and flexibly. "The different measures appropriate to the nine varieties of ground and the expediency of advance or withdrawal in accordance with circumstances and the fundamental laws of human nature are matters that must be studied carefully by a general." This is the most important philosophical thinking running through *The Art of War*. All methods are means and to defeat the enemy is the only goal. In order to realize this goal, any means can be used in any way, and we have to adapt the means to changes practically. It is under the guidance of this dialectic military philosophy that Sun Tzu raises the bold theory of "Throw them into a perilous situation and they will survive; put them in desperate ground and they will live." This theory is absolutely not to risk the soldiers' lives, for Sun Tzu is not an adventurist. He points out that it is the last resort when the troops are in the nine dangerous situations. Its role is positive. In short, what Sun Tzu means is that in a sense, death is the most powerful drive in war. It can trigger the power of life to seek survival and victory and thus break out of the adversity in war. It is usually a general rule of survival that "men survive in disasters and perish in comfort"

This chapter is also of immeasurable guiding value to business war. I think in the context of the integration of global economy, if we want to set up enterprises in a foreign country, we have to fully understand the international laws, and since our entry into the WTO, we should know more about the international trade laws, investment laws, intellectual property protection laws and laws on investment attracting. Only by know about these can we give full play to our potential in the international business. This is the inspiration from The Art of War. Only by making use of this wisdom can we develop an enterprise well.

The reason why foreigners come to invest in China is that they see the vast market and cheap labor in China. And we Chinese invest overseas because we are optimistic about the foreign resources including human capital and raw material resources. Any country, large or small, rich or poor, has its own advantages and disadvantages. And our policy is to "adopt its advantages and avoid its disadvantages."

11.4 Cases

Case 1

There are nine varieties of ground in war and the situation in business war is even more complicated. Therefore, if we can apply the experience in war of making use of ground to win victory to enterprise management, it is a creative study and application of the operational principles in art of war.

Tiananmen Square is regarded as a holy land in our homeland. Everything that happens to it attracts the world's attention. The development of Luohe Meat Packing Industry affiliated to Chinachem Shineway Group has benefited from Tiananmen the precious place.

Early in the morning on June 28, 1994, the Tiananmen Square was full of colored flags fluttering with a deafening sound of gongs and drums. The yangko team, stilt team and gong and drum team attracted people from all directions to come by and stop to watch. Tiananmen Square was packed all around. At 9 a.m. when leaders of the China's Communist Party and the state and leaders of Beijing announced that "Visit Beijing, Love Beijing and Build Beijing" large tourist cultural activity is opening, thousands of doves were released to fly into the skies, which led people's attention to sky. And they were surprised to see a dozen of large bright-colored balloons trailing a long banner read "Chinachem Shineway Group Luohe Meat Packing Plant Wishes the Activity a Great Success." What a spectacle as the banner swung in the wind! As the camera lens moved, this slogan flew to the television station via which it flew to millions of households. On July 15, *Henan Daily* published a 800-word front page news under a large headline: Shineway Fly High on Tiananmen. This report had triggered a ripple effect in many news media. The biggest beneficiary of the hype by the media was Chinachem Shineway Group Luohe Meat Packing Plant. Soon its popularity rose up in China or even in the world and it developed smoothly with the output value and the profit and taxes increasing each year. Now, it has grown into a national first-level enterprise with an annual output value of tens of millions of yuan.

Case 2

Sun Tzu said: "It is the business of a general to be quiet and thus ensure depth in deliberation; impartial and upright, and thus keep a good management."

Leaders at all levels in our institute should "be quiet and thus ensure depth in deliberation; impartial and upright, and thus keep a good management" when leading the employees to carry out all kinds of tasks.

Chairman Mao used to teach us that "cadres are a decisive factor, once a political line is decided." It is due to the locomotive that a train can run fast. And cadres are the locomotive that leads the staff forward. Sun Tzu requires a military officer to "be quiet and thus ensure depth in deliberation; impartial and upright, and thus keep a good management." It is the business of a general to calm down the troops with his own foresight and make them and upright with strict and impartial military discipline. In this way, the troops can strictly follow the commands and thus become invincible.

Our institute requires our leaders to be equipped with this quality, to use their uprightness to influence the staff and also the factories so that they can better cooperate with us to finish tasks.

For example, when we were performing a task in Tiansheng Thermal Power Plant, as the project time was very short and the task was heavy, under the guidance of the leader, our staff worked for consecutive nights and their eyes were bloodshot. Their spirit of dedication had moved the leaders of the factory who went to visit them many times and reminded them to pay more attention to safety in work. The leaders of the factory reported the performance of our staff to us immediately and asked us to reward them. To use the standard of a good military officer to require the leaders is to apply the thinking on military management in The Art of War to enterprise management and it also bears fruits. Just as the old Chinese saying goes that if the upper beam is not straight, the lower one will go aslant.

Case 3

Sun Tzu said: "In respect of the employment of troops, ground may be classified as dispersive, frontier, key, open, focal, serious, difficult, encircled, and desperate."

It seems to us that as there are nine varieties of ground in military, there are also nine grounds at the construction site. Accidents may happen if we act rashly without discriminating the construction site and investigating and doing research. For the past twenty years, our institute has been paying attention to conducting investigation on the construction site, conditions and facilities, for in this way we can work freely. It is just like one has to be familiar with the field if he wants to play football there and one has to know the depth of water before swimming there, we have to be familiar with our construction site before carrying out work there. It is similar to that the general has to know the battlefield before conducting operations in war.

Experience has proved that he who is not familiar with ground will suffer a great deal.

For instance, in 2009 a large-scale power plant in Dehui in the northeast of China asked us to carry out construction there. As we found potential safety hazard there after conducting a field investigation, we put forward that we will only enter the site to construct after rectifying it within a specified period. Particularly, we pointed out that the construction scaffolds did not meet the requirements of construction and had to be strengthened, otherwise they were not safe. And we could not enter the construction site if it was not safe. This principle of carrying out construction reflects our principle of human orientation. The usual way we do is that to see whether the construction site is safe by investigating the site. If it is not safe, we will leave the site. After conducting many investigations, we found that there are too many potential safety hazards in that power plant. Thus we left. It is our principle of construction that if we do it, we have to ensure the safety, otherwise, we quit.

After conducting many field investigations in the power plant, our construction leader found there were many safety hazards, especially the scaffolds particularly insecure and the bottom of the boiler not cleared.

Therefore, we left. However, another project team came to undertake the construction. Due to its carelessness in not examining the safety hazards, in the process of construction, a scaffold 30 meters high collapsed as the scaffold itself was not solid and its top is overloaded. It caused two workers to fall from the scaffold, one killed on the spot and another seriously injured with his legs broken, his face scratched and became disabled. What a horrible consequence! Such a lesson must never be forgotten!

In fact, safety is the most direct productivity. As we deem safety as the life of an enterprise and consider people's life and health as our top priority, safety has brought us benefit. Our institute has won Excellent Chinese Enterprise Award and The Scientific Achievements Award of The World Productivity (China).

Scientific achievements are made through hard work and sweat.

-Author's note

Chapter 12
ATTACK BY FIRE

This chapter discusses the object, condition and ways of attacking by fire and emphasizes the combat thinking of being cautious. Only by investigating the battlefield and laying out thorough plans before attacking by fire can one take the initiative.

Sun Tzu said: There are five ways of attacking with fire. The first is to burn soldiers in their camp[1]; the second, to burn provision and stores[2]; the third, to burn baggage-trains[3]; the fourth, to burn arsenals and magazines[4]; and the fifth, to burn the lines of transportation[5]. To use fire, some medium must be relied upon. Materials for setting fire must always be at hand[6]. There are suitable seasons to attack with fire, and special days for starting a conflagration[7]. The suitable seasons are when the weather is very dry; the special days are those when the moon is in the constellations of the Sieve, the Wall, the Wing or the Cross-bar[8]; for when the moon is in these positions there are likely to be strong winds all day long.

Now, in attacking with fire, one must respond to the five changing situations[9]: When fire breaks out in the enemy's camp, immediately coordinate your action from without[10]. If there is an outbreak of fire, but the enemy's soldiers remain calm, bide your time and do not attack. When the force of the flames has reached its height[11], follow it up with an attack[12], if that is practicable; if not, stay where you are. If fires can be raised from outside the enemy's camps, it is not necessary to wait until they are started inside. To attack with fire only when the moment is suitable[13]. If the fire starts from up-wind, do not launch attack from down-wind[14]. When the wind continues blowing during the day, then it is likely to die down at night. Now, the army must know the five different fire-attack situations and wait for appropriate times[15].

Those who use fire to assist their attacks can achieve tangible results[16]; those who use inundations can make their attacks more powerful. Water can intercept and isolate an enemy, but cannot deprive him of the supplies or equipment.

Now, to win battle and capture lands and cities, but to fail to consolidate these achievements is ominous[17] and may be described as a waste of resources and time[18]. And, therefore, the enlightened rulers must deliberate upon the plans to go to battle, and good generals carefully execute them. If not in the interests of the state, do not act[19]. If you are not sure of success, do not use troops[20]. If you are not in danger, do not fight a battle[21]. A sovereign should not launch a war simply out of anger, nor should a general fight a war simply out of resentment. Take action if it is to your advantage; cancel the action if it is not. An angered man can become happy again, just as a resentful one can feel pleased again, but a state that has perished can never revive, nor can a dead man be brought back to life. Therefore, with regard to the matter of war, the enlightened ruler is prudent, and the good general is full of caution[22]. Thus, the state is kept secure and the army preserved.

12.1 Notes

1. Burn soldiers in their camp: burn the enemy's soldiers and horses.

2. Burn provision and stores: burn the enemy's food and forage.

3. Burn baggage-trains: burn the enemy's impedimenta.

4. Burn arsenals and magazines: burn the enemy's warehouses of supplies.

5. Burn the lines of transportation: burn the enemy's supply line.

6. Materials for setting fire must always be at hand: things for setting fire must be prepared at all times.

7. There are suitable seasons to attack with fire, and special days for starting a conflagration: one has to choose the right time to attack by fire.

8. The Sieve, the Wall, the Wing or the Cross-bar: four of the twenty eight constellations in ancient China.

9. One must respond to the five changing situations: one must use the troops to deal with the changes in the enemy's situation caused by attacking with fire in time.

10. Immediately coordinate your action from without: let the troops outside to coordinate with the troops inside early. In other words, attack the enemy both from inside and outside.

11. When the force of the flames has reached its height: let the fire blaze to the greatest extent.

12. Follow it up with an attack: here it means attacking with troops.

13. Attack with fire only when the moment is suitable: attack with fire according to the climate and the phase of the moon.

14. If the fire starts from up-wind, do not launch attack from down-wind: up-wind means the direction the wind blows from, and down-wind the direction the wind goes towards.

15. Wait for appropriate times: wait for the time to be ripe.

16. Those who use fire to assist their attacks can achieve tangible results: obvious results have been achieved by attacking with fire.

17. To win battle and capture lands and cities, but to fail to consolidate these achievements is ominous: disasters might be invited if one does not consolidate the fruits of victory.

18. May be described as a waste of resources and time: a waste of money.

19. If not in the interests of the state, do not act: do not act if there is no advantage.

20. If you are not sure of success, do not use troops: do not send troops if victory is not ensured.

21. If you are not in danger, do not fight a battle: do not engage in a battle unless at a critical juncture.

22. Therefore, with regard to the matter of war, the enlightened ruler is prudent, and the good general is full of caution: thus a wise sovereign must be cautious and an able and virtuous general must be vigilant.

12.2 Explanation

Sun Tzu said: There are five objects to attack with fire: the enemy's men and horses, his provisions, impedimenta, warehouse and lines of transportation.

To attack with fire, some conditions must be met and the materials for setting fire must be all set. Before setting fire, one should choose the right weather and time. The weather the day one sets fire must be dry and the time should be when the moon is in one of the four constellations: the Sieve, the Wall, the Wing and the Cross-bar, for whenever the moon is passing by these four constellations, it is time for a strong wind.

To attack the enemy with fire, you have to flexibly use troops to support according to the following five changing situations. If you set fire within the enemy's camp, you should sent troops to cooperate from the outside in time. If the enemy's camp is already on fire yet the enemy remains calm, you should wait and see and never attack immediately. Make your decision according to the situation when the force of the flames has reached its height. If the situation allows an attack, attack, otherwise stop attacking. You can also set fire outside the camp so that you do not have to have someone to cooperate with you from inside. As long as the time is right, you can attack the enemy with fire. When setting fire, you should set it from upwind rather than from downwind. The wind lasts long during the day and stops at night. All generals must know the differences between the above five ways of attacking with fire and wait for the right time according to the law of changes in weather and climate.

Remarkable results can be achieved by using fire to assist military attack. Though using water can also enhance the military attack for it can obstruct the enemy's formation, communication and transportation, it cannot destroy his soldiers, horses and military supplies as fire does.

It is dangerous if one cannot consolidate his fruits of victory after winning battle and capture the enemy's land. It is called "a wasted of resources and time." thus, a wise sovereign should cautiously think about this problem and a good general should carefully deal with it. Do not act if there is no advantage; do not send troops if you are not sure of success; do not start a war unless you are in danger. A sovereign should not wage a war out of anger and a general, nor should a general fight a war out resentment. As long as it is in the interest of the state, send troops, otherwise, stop your action. An angry man can become happy again and a resentful one can feel pleased again. But a state that has perished will never revive just as no dead man can come back to life.

Therefore, a wise sovereign should be prudent with war and an excellent general should be vigilant about it. It is an important principle of keeping the state secure and maintaining the army sound.

12.3 Analysis

This chapter discusses the object, condition and ways of attacking by fire and emphasizes the thinking of being cautious.

There are five objects of attacking with fire: men, provisions, impedimenta, warehouse and lines of transportation. There are four conditions of attacking by fire: medium, materials, weather and time. Medium is a must in attacking with fire. It is complicated, for it is about whether we can attack the enemy with fire. If the conditions do not suit, then we cannot attack the enemy with fire. Therefore, before attacking with fire, we have to make field investigation and then start to make careful plan so that we can take the initiative and adopt attacking with fire as an auxiliary means. Otherwise, we will be landed in a passion position.

We have to take the operational method corresponding to the object of attack, for the situation on the battlefield changes all the time. The advice is really good and clear that "if the fire starts from up-wind, do not launch attack from down-wind."

"Consolidate achievements" is an important part in this chapter. We should consolidate our achievements and reward the soldiers after winning the victory. Only by rewarding them in time can the morale be inspired and thus be in the interest of the security of the state and the army.

Sun Tzu once again stresses being cautious about war and that the only aim of war is to get advantages. "If not in the interests of the state, do not act. If you are not sure of success, do not use troops. If you are not in danger, do not fight a battle." We should never wage a war out of personal dislike, personality or resentment. An angry man can be happy again and a resentful one can be pleased again. But a perished state can never be revived just as a dead person will never come back to life. He warns us that we should be cautious and vigilant about war.

The theme of "*Attacking by Fire*" is the way how to operate troops to win victories by borrowing strength. There are many situations that we can make use of to win victories: fire, water, wind, rain, night, terrain, weather, cold, screen, forest, crops and caves. In short, anything that is advantageous to war can be used in order to defeat the enemy and save ourselves.

This chapter is also of significant guiding value to business war. In business war, it is not about mechanically setting fire. It is about using the methods of borrowing strengths in *Attacking by Fire* to overwhelm the rivals and thus win the victory in business war. Methods of borrowing strengths in business war include inviting stars to advertise, name a football team, a cultural relic, a celestial star, a spaceship, an important building by sponsoring them to expand its influence and increase its publicity and thus achieve the best effects of advertising.

12.4 Cases

Case 1

The Parker pen has always enjoyed a great reputation in the world as a great writing instrument. Having a Parker pen is a symbol of identity and status. And the Parker Company also has prospered and earned a good reputation all over the world due to its high-quality Parker pens.

Between 1943 and 1944, WWII had entered the hardest phase. Parker presented to the Allied Forces' Commander in chief in the European War Zone General Eisenhower a tailor-made Parker pen the value of which was that the penholder was embedded with four pure gold made stars that symbolized his four-star military title. Its main purpose was to praise and extol the glorious achievements General Eisenhower had made and his great contribution to world peace during the WWII.

Two years later, the Allied Forces finally won a complete victory and it was this Parker pen embedded with four gold stars that General Eisenhower used to sign on the Capitulation of the Nazi Germany.

In March, 1972, Kissinger visited China and later the US President Nixon paid an official visit to China. President Nixon presented Chairman Mao Zedong a Parker pen the material of which included the dust of the moon brought back after the "Apollo" spaceship landed on the moon.

In December, 1987, the pens former US President Regan and former Soviet Union's General Secretary Mikhail Gorbachev used to sign *Elimination of Intermediate-Range and Long-Range Missiles* were also tailor-made by Parker. Both pens were made by pure silver engraved with Reagan's and Mikhail Gorbachev's name respectively. After signing on the treaty, both exchanged their own Parker pen as a souvenir.

The fact that the above mentioned ambassadors had used Parker pens to sign in world's important events had greatly improved Parker's publicity in the world. On the other hand, it fully displayed the significant position of Parker in the world's writing instruments. With a countless number of famous pen brands in the world, only Parker had the special honor to contact the world's influential men and it was just the sign of the prosperity of Parker.

With advertisements spread all over, like which one belongs to you and how to make your company another Parker? This is what all enterprises should strive to be.

Case 2

Ningbo Golden Eagle Group, an obscure enterprise, bid for the pair of out-of-use palace lanterns on Tiananmen gate tower with 13.8 million yuan, which was incomprehensible to many people. Whether it was worth ten million yuan to buy a pair of palace lanterns had become a concern of people after the auction.

In early March, the trees in Beijing had not sprouted. In the morning mist above the vast expanse between the Summer Palace and the hot spring to its west loomed a large archaized architectural complex. This is China Baitingyu Paradise---a high-end playground built in Beijing with an investment of 500million yuan by Ningbo Golden Eagle Group. The two red palace lanterns hung on the unfinished tower. Perhaps it was because they were for the first time hung in somewhere else other than Tiananmen, it made people feel particularly honored.

The Golden Eagle Group had become the new owner of the palace lanterns. More surprisingly, the Golden Eagle Group is a start-up the average age of whose staff was only 35, yet it operated hundreds of millions of yuan worth asset. Its President Wu Biao, who has a financial background, had led the enterprise to make a mark in industry, trade, real asset, finance, tourism and media within two years. China Baitingyu Paradise was the largest project in Beijing invested by Zhejiang Province.

When being asked by the journalist why he would be so obsessed with the palace lanterns, Wu Biao said: "First of all, we believe that this pair of palace lanterns is an invaluable treasure in China's cultural relics. They are witnesses of the history of the New China. When China Baitingyu Paradise is completed, we are going to hang them at the gate of the playground to let tourists visit them. As a powerful group, Golden Eagle Groups has the duty to protect our country's cultural relics."

The scenery in Baitingyu Paradise is really fantastic: tall and magnificent city gate tower, a black and white cottage built by the water. It is just like a beautiful landscape painting of the regions south of the Yangtze River. The 1,400-meter veranda, a hundred pavilions and glass enhancing each other's beauty, a long fresco of the 5000-year history of China and 1,080 stone tablets of the origins of the surnames in China are all fresh and new. And the red palace lanterns have finally found a new home.

The Golden Eagle Group was so obsessed with the palace lanterns not only out of the need of the architectural style of the paradise itself but also more out of the patriotic feeling of protecting cultural relics. However, to a businessman, buying palace lanterns is an investment. Thus, the effects it had generated include economic consequence as well as political, cultural and social ones. The Golden Eagle Group had exchanged a huge amount of money for more reward.

Someone had made the following calculations:

Since China Garter International Auction Company had announced to the media on January 9th that a pair of old palace lanterns on Tiananmen tower was to be auctioned off till the lanterns were successfully sold on February 19th, about 400 to 500 media home and abroad had reported it. If the Golden Eagle Group had paid these media for advertisement, it would cost it hundreds of millions of yuan. It is no wonder that some said that compared with paying to advertise, the successful bidding for the old-styled palace lanterns on Tiananmen tower is excellent, both money-saving and widespread in publicity.

What Golden Eagle Group people could feel obviously was that their business got much better. People indisputably trusted the strength of the Golden Eagle. Before the auction, Golden Eagle once wanted to buy steel from a large steel plant in Shanghai. But as the plant knew nothing about the credit position of this new client, the two did not sign a contract. Yet after the auction, when Golden Eagle went to Shanghai for the second time, hearing that it was the company that had bought the palace lanterns, the plant signed the contract without more ado. Recently, Golden Eagle intended to develop its business in Beijing and therefore wanted to find a place to build its headquarters building in Beijing. However, no new infrastructural projects would be approved again in the near future. There was a large joint-stock company in Beijing that had an approved project. But as it lacked fund, the project was unable to be started. Hearing that the enterprise that had bought the palace lanterns wanted to cooperate, the company negotiated with Golden Eagle soon about the collaboration. Bidding for the palace lanterns had won for the enterprise unexpected market advantages the business value of which is rather considerable.

After bidding for the palace lanterns, Golden Eagle Group had received much information that many companies want to cooperate with it. For instance, several prestigious hotels and restaurants in Guangzhou and Shanghai were willing to rent the red palace lanterns with a price of 30,000 yuan per day. If calculating with this price, Golden Eagle can get 10 million yuan each year without doing anything. But Wu Biao flatly refused them all for the reason that he would assure the people that he would take care of the palace lanterns and that Golden Eagle would never use the national treasure in pure business activities.

Insiders estimated that this pair of red palace lanterns is itself of high value of cultural relics and its value will increase each year.

The effect of palace lanterns reflects the wisdom of business competition in culture and the plentiful fruits of business planning and management.

The Golden Eagle people believed that if the palace lanterns, bought at the price of 13.8 million yuan, had been bought at a lower price, it would have fallen flat. On the surface, money was saved. But in fact, it meant failure. The positive effect brought by that was they priced it at around 20 million yuan but the palace lanterns could be considered priceless. This is part of the market strategy of flexibly applying the principle of borrowing strength in "*Attacking with Fire*" in *The Art of War.*

Case 3

Sun Tzu said: "Those who use fire to assist their attacks can achieve tangible results; those who use inundations can make their attacks more powerful." Both attacking with fire and water are ways of using strength to defeat the enemy.

Similarly, our institute's increase in reputation is not only due to our innovation but also the reports in media. The dozens of publicity reports in newspaper and magazines helped to increase our prestige. Especially the live spot coverage of me on the program "Struggle" on CCTV had boosted our institute's fame. Since the spot coverage on CCTV, there was a remarkable increase in the number of people who called me or wrote to me to negotiate business. It was obvious that our business went better and our friends increased. This is the importance of borrowing strength. *Grass Boat Trap for Arrows* of Romance of the Three Kingdoms shows the strength borrowing from external cause defeated the enemy.

Many people we did not know called us to cooperate with us or ask for technical service or consultation.

Ever since the report on CCTV, I constantly received hundreds of letters and almost received calls to ask for cooperation every day.

All these calls and letters involved the intention to cooperate with our institute in technical service. And our partners gradually increased. In order to meet more factories' demands of technical service, we bought another three large mechanization equipment to expand our institute and bring more benefits to our institute.

Case 4

As the saying goes, "fire and water have no mercy." A big fire can swallow the enemy's provisions, military supplies and materials. It can also destroy plants, equipment and properties.

The weapons our institute use include electric arc spraying gun, flame plating gun and carbon arc gun, all related to fire. The temperature of their flames all reaches above 2000°C. Any carelessness in using them will lead to fire accidents and cause great irreparable damage to people's lives and properties.

Sun Tzu said: "To use fire, some medium must be relied upon. Materials for setting fire must always be at hand. There are suitable seasons to attack with fire, and special days for starting a conflagration." It clearly tells us that there must be medium and conditions of using fire. It is of practical value to understand what Sun Tzu said about the medium of using fire from the view of safe production and avoiding fire accidents. At the construction site, apart from our institute, there are also other trades and industries. So there are a great deal of inflammable materials even oxygen and acetylene. Thus, it requires us to be careful. Any negligence might invite disaster.

For instance, in a plant in Jinan in 2009, electric welding sparks fell downstairs from a crack. While at that time, there lived dozens of migrant laborers downstairs and some of them were sound asleep. The spark ignited the inflammable plastic which in turn ignited the cotton in the quilt. Soon, a big fire was caused. Some migrant laborers were choked to death and two who were on night shift were burned to death as the fire intensified because a great number of inflammable foam plastics ignited. This disastrous lesson is a result of the fact that they failed to find out the fire accident hazard due to the ignorance of the fact of there must be medium of using fire. From the view of safety, it is not suitable for migrant laborers to live in a disordered construction site. If they had not lived there, no one would have died and nobody's life would have been in danger. This lesson must draw the attention of the leader at the construction site.

In our many years of practice, we have summed up the following valuable experience: first, separate the gas tanks of oxygen and acetylene at least five meters in between before flame plating; secondly, clear away inflammable materials at the construction site before igniting. No inflammable materials should be present anywhere the spark can reach; thirdly, no smoking at the construction site. Anyone caught smoking at the site will be fined 100 yuan. After the constant safety education for years, our staff checks for safety before construction, pays attention to safety in construction and clears the site after construction, leaving no safety hazard. Though dealing with fire all the time, our institute has never encountered a fire accident. It tells us that as long as we pay attention to safety, accidents can be avoided. For the sake of people's life and properties, we must be prudent and careful!

As we have made safety first and managed appropriately, in 2003, our institute won China Excellent Enterprise Database Certificate of Honor issued by China Enterprise Confederation and China Enterprise Directors Association.

To struggle makes your life so colorful.

-Author's note

Chapter 13
USE OF SPIES

This chapter is the last one in The Art of War. It is about an important strategy of knowing the enemy and knowing yourself. It is about the key link of winning a battle. It is the earliest work on intelligence in China and the world.

Sun Tzu said: Generally, when an army of one hundred thousand is raised and dispatched on a distant war, the expenses borne by the people together with the disbursements made by the treasury will amount to a thousand dollars per day. There will be continuous commotion both at home and abroad; people will be involved with convoys and exhausted from performing transportation services[1], and seven hundred thousand households[2] will be unable to continue their farmwork[3]. Hostile armies confront each other for years[4] in order to struggle for victory in a decisive battle; yet if one who begrudges the expenditure of one hundred dollars in honors and emoluments[5] remains ignorant of his enemy's situation, he is completely devoid of humanity. Such a man is no leader of the troops[6]; no capable assistant to his sovereign; no master of victory[7]. Now, the reason that the enlightened sovereign and the wise general conquer the enemy whenever they move and their achievements surpass those of ordinary men[8] is that they have foreknowledge. This 'foreknowledge' cannot be elicited from spirits, or from gods, or by analogy with past events[9], or by any deductive calculation[10]. It must be obtained from the men who know the enemy situation.

Hence, the use of spies, of whom there are five sorts: native spies[11], internal spies, converted spies, doomed spies, and surviving spies. When all these five sorts of spies are at work and none knows their method of operation, it would be divinely intricate[12] and constitutes the greatest treasure of a sovereign[13]. Native spies are those we employ from the enemy's country people[14]. Internal spies are enemy official whom we employ[15]. Converted spies are enemy spies whom we employ[16]. Doomed spies are those of our own spies who are deliberately given false information[17] and told to report it to the enemy[18]. Surviving spies are those who return from the enemy camp to report information.

Hence, of all those in the army close to the commander, none is more intimate than the spies[19]; of all rewards, none more liberal than those given

187

to spies[20]; of all matters, none is more confidential than those relating to spying operations[21]. He who is not sage cannot use spies. He who is not humane and generous cannot use spies. And he who is not delicate and subtle cannot get the truth out of them. Delicate indeed! Truly delicate! There is no place in which espionage is not possible. If plans relating to spying operations are prematurely divulged[22] the spy and all those to whom he spoke of them should be put to death[23].

Generally, whether it is armies that you wish to strike[24], cities that you wish to attack, and individuals that you wish to assassinate, it is necessary to find out the names of the garrison commander, the aides-de-camp, the ushers, gatekeepers, and body-guards[25]. You must instruct your spies to ascertain these matters in minute detail.

The enemy's spies who have come to spy on us must be sought out[26], tempted with bribes[27], led away and comfortably housed. Thus they will become converted spies and available for our service. It is through the information brought by the converted spies[28] that native and internal spies can be recruited and employed[29]. It is owing to their information, again, that the doomed spies, armed with false information, can be sent to convey it to the enemy. Lastly, it is by their information that the surviving spies can come back and give information as scheduled. The sovereign must have full knowledge of the activities of the five sorts of spies. And to know these depends upon the converted spies. Therefore, it is mandatory that they be treated with the utmost liberality[30].

In ancient times, the rise of the Shang Dynasty[31] was due to Yi Zhi, who had served under the Xia[32]. Likewise, the rise of the Zhou Dynasty[33] was due to Lv Ya[34], who had served under the Yin. Therefore, it is only the enlightened sovereign and the wise general who are able to use the most intelligent people as spies and achieve great results. Spying operations are essential in war; upon them the army relies to make its every move[35].

13.1 Notes

1. Exhausted from performing transportation services: the people are tired due to long time transportation.

2. Continue their farm work: do farm work.

3. Seven hundred thousand households: it means the great impact of military operations on normal farming families.

4. Hostile armies confront each other for years: the two in stalemate for many years.

5. If one who begrudges the expenditure of one hundred dollars in honors and emoluments: if one does not use spies due to his stinginess on title, salary and money.

6. Such a man is no leader of the troops: the general who knows nothing about using spies to carry out special tasks is not a good leader that can lead the troops.

7. No capable assistant to his sovereign; no master of victory: not a good sovereign that can lead the troops so victory in battle.

8. Conquer the enemy whenever they move: defeat the enemy once he sends the troops.

9. (This 'foreknowledge' cannot be elicited) by analogy with past events: one should not know the enemy's situation by imagination.

10. By any deductive calculation: cannot know the enemy's situation in the same way to verify the degrees of the movement of the sun and the moon.

11. Native spies: to get into the enemy's camp for intelligence by making use of the fact that he is a countryman of the enemy's officer.

12. Divinely intricate: mysterious way

13. The greatest treasure of a sovereign: the magic key to a sovereign's victory in a battle.

14. Native spies are those we employ from the enemy's country people: make use of his identity as the countryman of the enemy's general to be a spy.

15. Internal spies are enemy official whom we employ: an internal spy is the enemy's officer who has been bought over.

16. Converted spies are enemy spies whom we employ: a converted spy is the enemy's spy who has been employed or bought off.

17. Those of our own spies who are deliberately given false information: deliberately spread the false intelligence in order to deceive the enemy.

18. Told to report it to the enemy: make our spy know about our deliberately spread false intelligence and tell the enemy's spy to trick the enemy into deception. After that, our spy cannot avoid to be executed to death, so we call such a spy doomed spy.

19. Hence, of all those in the army close to the commander, none is more intimate than the spies: the most trusted man in the whole army is a spy.

20. Of all rewards, none more liberal than those given to spies: spies can be rewarded more that any others.

21. Of all matters, none is more confidential than those relating to spying operations: of all military confidentialities, nothing is more secret than spying operations.

22. If plans relating to spying operations are prematurely divulged: before the plan of using spies are carried out.

23. The spy and all those to whom he spoke of them should be put to death: if the spying operation is exposed, the spy and the insider have to be killed.

24. Armies that you wish to strike: the enemy you wish to attack.

25. The garrison commander, the aides-de-camp, the ushers, gatekeepers, and body-guards: the commanding general, trusted men of the commanding general, officers responsible for delivering information, gate-keeper and advisory officer.

26. The enemy's spies who have come to spy on us must be sought out: we must find out the enemy's spies who come to conduct spying operations in our camp.

27. Tempted with bribes: take the advantage to buy off and employ the

enemy's spy.

28. It is through the information brought by the converted spies: get information from the converted spy.

29. That native and internal spies can be recruited and employed: we can better use our native spies and internal spies by employing converted spies.

30. Therefore, it is mandatory that they be treated with the utmost liberality: thus we should treat the converted generously.

31. The Shang Dynasty: it is called Yin for it moved from Shangqiu County to Yin.

32. Yi Zhi, who had served under the Xia: Yi Zhi used to be an officer serving Xia Jie. Later, he went to serve Shang Tang. In the process of destroying Xia, Yi Zhi had played an important role. Xia is the first slavery dynasty in China by the son of Da Yu Zi Xia. It was destroyed by Shang Tang when it was under the reign of Xia Jie.

33. Zhou Dynasty: the dynasty established by Emperor Wu after he destroyed Shang in 11 B.C.

34. Lv Ya: Master Keung. He used to be the officer of Emperor Zhou of Yin. When Emperor Wu of Zhou attacked Zhou, he appointed Master Keung as general and successfully defeated Emperor Zhou.

35. Spying operations are essential in war; upon them the army relies to make its every move: the troops have to conduct operations according to the intelligence provided by spies.

13.2 Explanation

Sun Tzu said: when a state wages a large-scale war by sending troops a thousand miles away, the people provide military supplies and the state has to spend a huge amount of money. Because of war, the number of farmers who cannot do farm work reaches seventy hundred thousand. We reach in a stalemate with the enemy in order to win the war. Therefore, those generals who begrudge money to buy spies to know the enemy's situation are not compassionate with his soldiers. Such men are not qualified to be generals, to the aides of a sovereign or the leaders of victory.

The reason why an enlightened sovereign and an excellent general can defeat the enemy once they send their troops is that they know the enemy's situation before dispatching their men. They never get to know the enemy's situation by believing the revelation of ghost or god, nor by making analogy with past events, nor by guessing with the degrees of the movement of the sun and the moon. They get the information from the one who really knows the enemy's situation.

There are five types of spies we can use: native spies, internal spies, converted spies, doomed spies, and surviving spies. By making use of the five spies at the same time, we can make the enemy feel at a loss about our means and methods of using spies and make them feel mysterious. This is the key to our defeating the enemy.

A native spy is an ordinary man among the enemy's residents. An internal spy is the enemy's officer who has been bought over to be our spy. A converted spy is the enemy's spy who worked for us. A doomed spy is the spy who makes false information to deceive the enemy (as such a spy will always be killed once the truth is found, hence the name). And a surviving spy is the spy that can come back alive to report the enemy's situation.

Thus, to the sovereign and the general who command the whole army and conduct the military operations, no man is more intimate than a spy in the entire army and no man is rewarded more than a spy, and the task is no more confidential that that of a spy. He who is not wise cannot use spies. He who is not humane and generous cannot use spies. And he who is not delicate and subtle cannot get the truth out of them. Delicate indeed! Truly delicate! There is no place in which espionage is not possible. If plans relating to spying operations are prematurely divulged the spy and all those to whom he spoke of them should be put to death.

To the enemy we want to strike, the city tower we wish to attack and the enemy's officer we want to assassinate, we should know in advance the name of the enemy's garrison general, his aides-de-camp, the officer in charge of communication and gate-keeping and the aides and staff. These are what our spies must scout out.

We must find out the enemy's spies who are spying on us and use privileged treatment and money to buy them over, give them task, let them go back and turn them into converted spies to be used by us. With the intelligence provided by converted spies, we can foster and use native spies and internal spies. With converted spies, the false information spread by doomed spies can be known by the enemy through converted spies and with converted spies, our surviving spies can come back to report the enemy's situation as scheduled. A sovereign must know clear and master the use of these five types of spies. And among the five types of spies, converted spies is the key. Therefore, the treatment of converted spies should also be the most privileged.

Previously, the rise of the Shang Dynasty owed a lot to the fact that Yi Zhi had served under the Xia and the rise of the Zhou Dynasty benefited a lot from the fact that Lv Ya had served under the Yin. Thus, an enlightened sovereign and a wise general who can use the most intelligent people as spies will surely achieve great success. Using spies are the secret of success in war and the whole army relies on the information provided by the spies to decide its military operations.

13.3 Analysis

This chapter is the last chapter in The Art of War. It is about an important strategy of knowing the enemy and knowing yourself. It is about the key link of winning a battle. It is a systematic summary of the rich experience in using spies by the ancients by Sun Tzu in theory. And it is an important mark of the basic formation of the ideological system of using spies in ancient China.

As spying operations requires great wisdom and abilities are very dangerous tasks for once exposed, spies will be killed, the expenses on spy training, activities and payment are very high. Without money, things cannot be completed. But some begrudge money to use spies. However, that is not what Sun Tzu believe in. from the view of the interests of the state and his people, he points out that a general will lose more if not he is not willing to use money on spying operations. It is a responsibility for the state and for the people's life and properties. It is the general's malpractice and shows his heartlessness.

Each type of spy is of its own use and has its own characteristics. "When all these five sorts of spies are at work and none know their method of operation, it would be divinely intricate and constitutes the greatest treasure of a sovereign." The comprehensive and flexible use of various ways of collecting intelligence is like a magic key the value of which is immeasurable.

The principles of using spies are intimacy, privileged treatment and confidentiality. And at the same one has to be wise, humane, generous and delicate. Sun Tzu points out: "He who is not sage cannot use spies. He who is not humane and generous cannot use spies. And he who is not delicate and subtle cannot get the truth out of them. Delicate indeed! Truly delicate!" "There is no place in which espionage is not possible. If plans relating to spying operations are prematurely divulged the spy and all those to whom he spoke of them should be put to death." They are practices of the principles of "that nothing is more confidential than those relating to spying operations." Confidentiality is the major characteristic of using spies. Sometimes, even the spy himself does not know the secret in a spying operation. Only the sovereign and the commander-in-chief know it.

The object of spying operations should be around the object the army wishes to strike, attack and kill, for example, the garrison general, his aide-de-camp, the officers in charge of delivering information, the gate-keeper and the advisory officer.

The rise of Yin and Zhou owes great to their respective use of the former officers in Xia and Shang Yi Zhi and Lv Ya, for they came from the enemy's camp and knew clearly the enemy's situation and thus could give full play to their role of knowing the enemy and knowing yourself.

The use of men and use of spies share the same principle. In any successful business, the really strong one can only defeat his enemy by knowing him and only can created new things by being familiar with the old ones.

Use of Spies is the earliest work on intelligence in China and the world. It is the most classic and most concise intelligence theory. Only by using the principle of using spies in The Art of War to study the strategic means used in business and enterprise management can one efficiently defeat the rivals.

13.4 Cases

Case 1

In the US Silicon Valley known as "High-tech Center," Company A which goes into online game software development used "use of spies" defeat its strong rival Company B.

In the middle of 1990s, online games were all the rage at the time. Developing game software became an extremely profitable industry. Back then, Company A was devoting itself to developing new global online game software called "Absolute Action." Just as the software was to finish, there came to its HR department an applicant called Frank who claimed that he was a doctor majoring in computer at the Massachusetts Institute of Technology and mainly engaged in game software development. Hearing this, its President John came to see him soon. However, during the conversation, Frank's evasive answers raised doubt in John. Though on the surface, he had approved Frank's application and appointed him to a position in the Software Development Department, he secretly sent people to investigate Frank's background. And finally he came to know that Frank was a commercial spy sent by Company B to get Company A's game software "Absolute Action."

Most of the Company A's senior managers advised to fire Frank immediately. But John got another idea. He pretended to not know Frank's true identity and gave the sample of "Absolute Action" to Frank on purpose but had set secretly a timed virus in the software. As expected, Frank left without notice and took the software back to Company B. Having changed the name of the game software, Company B soon launched it in the market. At first, it was exceptionally salable. But just as Company B was pleased with itself and waiting to profit, the secret virus set by Company A broke out. And soon the vendors of this software suffered a lot. And all vendors rallied together to attack Company B. They not only filed a claim against Company B, but also decided not to buy any game software made by Company B. Finally, Company B ended in obscurity when besieged on all sides. Although they lost the new game software "Absolute Action," by using spies, Company A had defeated its strong rival and its business prospered gradually.

Case 2

Chocolate candy is almost everybody's love. It is said that the well-known French Emperor Napoleon also loved chocolate very much. Whenever he went out to battle, he would asked his aide-de-camp to bring large packs of chocolate. And when he was exhausted or overstrained his nerves, he would put some chocolate in his mouth.

The main raw material to make chocolate is cocoa which grows mostly in Central America and the south of Mexico. By drying the seeds of cocoa, peeling them and grinding them, the raw material of making chocolate is obtained. The Maya in ancient Mexico called cocoa the tree of life. Every time a baby was born, they would plant a cocoa to wish a healthy growth to the new-born baby. They believed that the fruit of cocoa symbolizes human heart and thus the drink made from it was blood and could bring people exuberant vigor.

The Mexican had long mastered the skill of making chocolate.

In the 14th Century, knowledge about chocolate was completely owned and managed by Mexico directly under the regulation of the nation. When the first Spanish colonial army arrived in Mexico, they found that the locals were drinking chocolate with relish. Someone tasted a sip and spit it out soon after it went into the mouth, yelling out: only pigs drink it. The reason is that the chocolate then is without sugar and vanilla.

In 1915, a Spanish Knight came to Mexico in the name of travelling around the world. Seeing him graceful and friendly, the hospital Mexicans broke a rule and agreed to let him visit the production line of chocolate. But the Mexicans would never have thought that this sanctimonious distinguished guest was a commercial spy. He was the first man who stole from Mexico the technology of making chocolate. Since then, the production of chocolate started in Spain and soon became a burgeoning food industry there. Many Spaniards had made a big fortune due to the production of chocolate, which made the businessmen in other European countries covet. They all went to Spain, in the hope of obtaining cannons. However, the Spaniard kept silent about the technology of making chocolate. And just like this, the Spanish technology of making chocolate became the important object of the industrial spies of other European countries.

In this war of espionage, the Italians were the first to succeed. In 1606, they bought with a large sum of money and stole the Spanish secret of producing chocolate, breaking Spanish monopoly in the production of chocolate. Soon, the British manufacturers followed suit and successfully stole the production formula in 1763. They improved the recipe boldly and produced milk chocolate, making Britain a chocolate tycoon. In 1800, industrial spies from Switzerland followed and stole the technology and made itself a world-renowned "Chocolate Kingdom." Meanwhile, manufacturers in Germany also stole the technology and made chocolate into candy and competed with other countries. Later, Japan also joined this espionage war of chocolate. The espionage war and trade war generated by Chocolate went on and off for a hundred of years and has not come to an end even today.

In 1981, Switzerland overtook the former Federal Republic of Germany and sold 280 thousand tons of chocolate to more than 100 countries, making itself the largest exporter of chocolate in the world. In Switzerland, the average chocolate consumed by each one per year is 10kg, ranking first in the world. In order to maintain its dominant role in producing and selling chocolate, Switzerland drew lessons from the ancients and stipulated in its law that anyone who sells economic information (including the technology of producing chocolate) reveals the absolute secrets of the nation, and shall be punished for treason. However, despite the strict law, there were still a large number of people willing to sell information as a spy due to the lure of money. At the beginning of 1980s, former Soviet Union kept sending industrial spies to Switzerland, hoping to steal its technology of producing chocolate. In 1982, after a long investigation, the police in Switzerland finally caught the tail of the spies sent by Soviet Union. They laid an ambush in a cafe and arrested a pack of industrial spies sent to steal the secret of producing chocolate. Two employees in a famous chocolate food factory that was about to sell 40 sheets of chocolate recipe to the Soviet Union's spies were caught on the spot.

Thus we can see that the espionage war in business war is no less than that in military war.

Case 3

Sun Tzu said: "Therefore, it is only the enlightened sovereign and the wise general who are able to use the most intelligent people as spies and achieve great results. Spying operations are essential in war; upon them the army relies to make its every move."

Every time we go to a new factory, we visit the leaders of the factory to let them know that we are sincere in cooperating with them, that we have high technology to serve them, that we are willing to make intimate friends with them, that we can improve their economies and that our contracts will increase constantly if we can make friends as powerful as them that are men of words. An enlightened sovereign and a wise general need to make friends with the most intelligent men to achieve great causes. Factory directors and senior engineers are not only wise and powerful, they will also speak for us in critical moment and they are men of words. Why wouldn't we make friends with them? We can benefit each other.

Once at a bidding spot, there were both high and low quotes. We were not sure how much to quote. Despite our high technology and good quality, we should not too high on the price. Just as we were at a loss and could not make the decision, a message popped up on my mobile phone---a senior engineer from the factory gave us the reference price. Thus, we won the bidding.

Making friends with such a friend reflects one's level.

"An enlightened sovereign and a wise general should make friends with the most intelligent."

Though not enlightened sovereigns or wise generals, leaders in our institute are first-class academicians and professors. Thus, of course we have to choose high-level and wise men to be our agents. For this purpose, in the name of our institute we have issued letters of appointment to the enterprises' senior leaders and experts to hire them as our real technology promoters and publicists. With such most intelligent men, we have obvious advantages in biddings and we can get a lot of construction tasks from all sides. The wisdom in The Art of War has made contributions to the development of our institute.

Case 4

Our Dalian Katelin Specific Alloy Institute is a high-tech enterprise with three invention patents and four proprietary intellectual property rights of high-tech achievements. To protect our intellectual property, all new employees have to first receive confidentiality education the day they come to work in the institute. It is clearly stipulated in the labor contract that you are not allowed to reveal the institute's secrets of technology nor are you allowed to serve other companies with our technology secrets. Shall such a thing happen, you should take legal action.

In spite of these terms, many economic spies try it themselves by offering high prices the business manager of our institute. And some spies offer to work for our institute at the construction site free of charge to spy on our secrets of technologies. Some also go to the construction site to find out information about our equipment and the formula of our raw materials. Some even get residues of our materials at the construction site for test and analysis so as to find out our secrets in the formula.

Responding to this, we strengthen the ideological education on our staff and offer them rich material rewards. We make them understand that the knowledge they master is due to the institute's elaborate training and thus that they should not do anything harmful to the institute. On the other hand, we offer them generous treatment so that they do not want to leave. In this way, we can maintain a stable technology power and enable the institute to have strong research and development capabilities and technology cadre team.

Our institute will not let go of the technology backbone a company wants to poach unless it pays our institute 300,000 yuan of technology training fee. Though some companies want our people, but 300,000 yuan is a large sum of money and they cannot afford it for the time being and thus dispel the idea. In a word, we do not allow other companies to poach our staff and neither do we allow our staff to hop. And these are the basic measures our institute adopt to protect our intellectual property.

During our construction, visit is not allowed. After the construction, the site should be cleared away and irrelevant persons are not allowed to be at the site to get residues of materials.

In China, the protection of intellectual property has a long way to go. Its major problem is people's weak legal awareness. They believe that stealing technology is not as bad as stealing money or property. But in fact, from the perspective of law, stealing technology is a serious theft and has to be brought to justice.

Since the day our institute was set up, we have been engaging ourselves in the fight of anti-spy and preventing spy. We pay patent fees to the state every year so that we can get legal protection from the state in case our intellectual property rights are infringed upon. In view of our outstanding achievements in translating our patents into productivity, the State Intellectual Property Office awarded our institute the honorary title of "One Hundred Outstanding Inventors at the 60th Anniversary of the Founding of New China" in October, 2009.

Know the enemy and know yourself, and you can fight a hundred battles with no danger of defeat. Men survive in disasters and perish in comfort.

-Author's note

BIBLIOGRAPHY

1. Compiling Group of A Dictionary of Ancient Chinese Characters in Common Use. *A Dictionary of Ancient Chinese Characters in Common Use*, The Commercial Press, 2003.

2. Compiling Group of A Dictionary of Ancient Chinese Characters in Common Use. *A Dictionary of Ancient Chinese Characters in Common Use* (large print edition), The Commercial Press, 2003.

3. Luo Guanzhong. *Romance of the Three Kingdoms*. Shanghai Classics Publishing House.

4. Sun Tzu. *The Art of War*. China Textile & Apparel Press, 2007.

5. Sun Tzu etc. *Wisdom in The Art of War and Thirty-Six Stratagems*. China Changan Publishing House, 2005.

6. Ma Jun. *Ma Jun Talking about The Art of War*. Zhonghua Book Company, 2008.

7. Yang Yi. *Comments and Annotations on The Art of War*. Yuelu Publishing House, 2006.

8. Sun Tzu. *The Art of War*. Jilin Publishing Group, 1999.

9. Chen Yunjin, Lu Baosheng. *Appreciate The Art of War*. Wuhan University Press, 2006.

10. Lv Shuchun. *Strategies in Business War and The Art of War*. China Logistics Publishing House, 2004.

11. He Shaohua. *The Art of War and The Art of Management*. Central South University Press, 2004.

POSTSCRIPT

Chairman Mao said: "The army without knowledge is a foolish one." *The Art of War* proves that how wise this statement is! As an excellent militarist, one has to be both knowledgeable and have deep philosophical thought and strategies to win victories in war.

In a broader sense, by perusing art of war and master military stratagems, an excellent entrepreneur can give full play to his talents freely in enterprise management and business war and finally becomes invincible. Everything in the universe communicates with each other. To learn philosophy and dialectics and to read carefully books on art of war are important means for today's entrepreneurs to master enterprise management. After sharing my experience in studying of *The Art of War* and my opinions on it with my old friend Professor Zhang Xiuyu, I won his support. He suggested I write about my many years of studying and practicing and publish a book not only to communicate with fans about the of art of war, but also to experts and scholars in enterprise management and to serve as a modest spur to induce others' valuable ideas.

As a member of China Association of Productivity Science, I deem the association as a warm family where there are many revered experts, scholars and leaders, such as Honorary President Yu Guanyuan, President Wang Maolin, Vice President Zhai Ligong, Secretary General Chen Shengchang and leaders and editors from publishing houses. Under their encouragement and support, I have always been hoping to do more for the association. With my best efforts, I have finished compiling my achievement of many years of research---*The Art of War and Enterprise Strategy Management*, finally doing something for the association. I hope that any expert, scholar and entrepreneur pursuing innovating enterprise management will refer to this book and give their valuable opinions on it, for which I will be very grateful in my entire life.

Fu Shouzhi

www.ingramcontent.com/pod-product-compliance
Lightning Source LLC
Chambersburg PA
CBHW061217220326
41599CB00025B/4667